Escaping the
Parent Trap

Escaping the
Parent Trap

14 PRINCIPLES FOR
A BALANCED FAMILY LIFE

DR. DEBBIE CHERRY

author of childproofing your marriage

LIFE JOURNEY®

Bringing Home the Message for Life

COOK COMMUNICATIONS MINISTRIES
Colorado Springs, Colorado • Paris, Ontario
KINGSWAY COMMUNICATIONS LTD
Eastbourne, England

Life Journey® is an imprint of
Cook Communications Ministries, Colorado Springs, CO 80918
Cook Communications, Paris, Ontario
Kingsway Communications, Eastbourne, England

ESCAPING THE PARENT TRAP
© 2006 Debbie L. Cherry, PhD

The Web addresses (URLs) recommended throughout this book are solely
offered as a resource to the reader. The citation of these Web sites does
not in any way imply an endorsement on the part of the author or the
publisher, nor does the author or publisher vouch for their content for
the life of this book.

Published in association with Yates and Yates, LLP, Attorneys and
Counselors, Orange, CA.

Cover Design: Two Moore Designs/Ray Moore
Cover Photo Credit: iStock

First printing, 2006
Printed in Canada.

1 2 3 4 5 6 7 8 9 10 Printing/Year 10 09 08 07 06

Library of Congress Cataloging-in-Publication Data

Cherry, Debbie L.
  Escaping the parent trap : 14 principles for a balanced family life /
Debbie L. Cherry.-- 1st ed.
    p. cm.
  ISBN 0-7814-4266-4
  1. Parenting--Religious aspects--Christianity. 2. Family--Religious life. I.
Title.
BV4529.C45 2006
649'.1--dc22
                    2005033381

To my four little "treasures,"

Taffeta, Tiara, Talon, and Trayton

Acknowledgments

જી

As always, thanks go first and foremost to God Almighty, who has continued to prove himself faithful in each and every aspect of my life!

To my loving and devoted husband, Jim, there are no words that can adequately express what you mean to me. You are the greatest treasure I could ever receive on this earth. Thank you for encouraging me to pursue my dreams and supporting me every step of the way.

A special thank-you goes out to all the wonderful people at Cook Communications. Thank you for believing in me and always making me look better than I ever thought possible. You're great!

To Chris Ferbee and everyone at Yates and Yates, Inc. Thank you for pushing me forward and knowing that I have so much more inside of me than I've put to paper so far. Your encouragement is not forgotten.

And finally, to the many parents who have shared their stories and struggles with me over the years. May God bless each of you beyond measure.

Contents

&

INTRODUCTION

Parenting, a.k.a "Survival of the Fittest"

Matt and Laura had been married only a few years and still felt like newlyweds. Of course, like most people, they experienced the stress of work, finances, and being constantly on the go. But they enjoyed their life together and had learned the key to staying close and connected through a treasure box they found on the beach a few years back. (For that story, see *Discovering the Treasure of Marriage*.) Their life was comfortable, and they had settled into a routine. They felt they had found the perfect balance between structure and spontaneity, organization and freedom, work and playtime.

And then, *it* happened ... and everything changed.

One day, Laura was casually flipping through the mail. Suddenly, her eyes widened, her face went pale, and she felt nauseous as she held the blue envelope. Although she expected this letter to come someday, today was definitely not the someday she had hoped for. Matt walked in and saw Laura's face and the blue envelope and he, too, knew what this meant. They hugged briefly and opened the letter. They had been selected to participate in the hottest reality show ever—*Parenting*, a.k.a.

"Survival of the Fittest." They learned they had just a few months to prepare before they had to report to the set of this challenging adventure. As the news sank in, they experienced a rush of mixed emotions: excitement, joy, fear, and anticipation. Regardless of when they'd hoped to volunteer for this challenge—and they *had* hoped to volunteer some distant day—now was the time. They would meet this challenge head-on.

IN THE BLINK OF AN EYE, THEIR ENTIRE WORLD TURNED UPSIDE DOWN AND INSIDE OUT.

They determined to spend the next few months doing everything possible to prepare for the challenge ahead. They read books about the challenge, they interviewed previous contestants, they made a list of supplies, and they prayed. They spent hours watching episodes of the game show hoping to gain some additional insight. From what they could tell, this was an all-encompassing challenge in a constantly changing environment. It required the contestants' total, 24/7 devotion for many, many years.

Although they didn't feel completely secure, Matt and Laura did feel they were better prepared than most contestants and could maneuver this challenge better than others they'd been watching.

The day arrived. In the blink of an eye, their entire world turned upside down and inside out. Through a powerful explosion of pain, joy, and tears, Matt and Laura were dropped smack dab into the most challenging survival environment ever—the jungle of parenting. They were thankful for the information they'd gleaned from their few months' study, but they were quickly humbled and realized that much of what they thought they knew really didn't make much sense in the actual jungle. No amount of training could have prepared them for this. They were told to "watch out for all the 'parent traps' out there and do the best you can with what you have!"—but what they had was practically nothing.

Matt and Laura surveyed their new environment and realized this jungle seemed slightly different from others they'd seen while watching the show. The host informed them that basic elements exist in all the jungles, but no two are exactly alike.

"This feature keeps contestants on their toes and makes the game even more challenging," he said. He further explained that even Matt and Laura's personal jungle would change if they began the game again because it's never the same thing twice.

As the couple explored the jungle, they found diapers and bottles in one area, baseballs and pogo sticks in another, and make-up and cars somewhere else. How could they ever survive in this ever-changing environment? At every turn there seemed to be new hazards. When they thought they had it figured out, the environment—and even the rules, such as who's in charge and how much control would bring the best outcome—changed again.

Matt and Laura's excitement at this new challenge quickly disappeared and was replaced with physical exhaustion and frustration. They had no map, no compass, no survival equipment. Before long, they were floundering just to stay alive one day at a time. The option of quitting wasn't available. They were sure they wouldn't survive this experience.

At last, the host appeared with two boxes—a small but beautiful treasure chest and a large wooden crate. Both were marked "Parents' Survival Kit" and both contained parenting "supplies." Matt and Laura could examine the containers without opening them, but then must choose one or the other—and their decision would be final.

Desperate for any kind of help, Matt and Laura rushed to the large crate and tried to lift it. It was so heavy that they couldn't even budge it. Both wanted the most possible help, and this huge trunk was obviously full of supplies. They talked about what could be inside; they needed survival essentials, but also were hoping for things to make their experience here more comfortable and satisfying. What they wanted most were the supplies needed to succeed through the game's many challenges.

As they were about to tell the host to open the crate, they remembered the ornate little treasure chest. Maybe they should at least look at it before choosing. As they passed it back and forth, Matt commented that it felt practically empty. But the case was so beautiful that it continued to capture their attention. Laura said, "It looks so much like the treasure chest we found on the beach years ago." They remembered the amazing treasure the other box held: the power to keep a marriage strong and growing for a lifetime. Could this little trinket hold the key to surviving the parenting jungle? They had to know. With great anticipation, they told the host, "We choose this one."

THEY REMEMBERED THE AMAZING TREASURE THE OTHER BOX HELD: THE POWER TO KEEP A MARRIAGE STRONG AND GROWING FOR A LIFETIME.

The host smiled and declared the decision final. Then he offered to show Matt and Laura what they had given up in the large crate. They didn't really want to see all the things they knew they needed and would now likely have to do without—yet they were dying to know. As the host lifted the lid, the excitement quickly faded at the sight of the "parenting supplies": roller skates, a basketball, the latest electronic game, and a wad of cash. The crate held a few basic supplies, but was filled mostly with trinkets and toys for children of all ages.

Matt and Laura looked on in disbelief. How could that stuff have helped them survive? With curiosity growing, they turned their attention to their little treasure chest. The host handed them the key, and with a quick prayer, they opened the lid. They reached in and pulled out an old, rolled-up piece of parchment. At first glance, it looked even more worthless than the contents of the big crate. They unrolled it and discovered it was a map. As they looked closer, they realized it was the map of *their* jungle. It marked some very important places they didn't even know existed and might never have discovered without this map. They couldn't wait to explore helpful oases such as the following:

> IT WAS SO SIMPLE AND CLEAR THAT IT ALMOST FELT LIKE "CHEATING."

- "The Fountain of Ever-Flowing Conversation" to drink from and quench their thirst
- "The Orchard of Effective Parenting Skills" to pick from and relieve their hunger
- "The Cabin of Wisdom from Scripture" to shelter themselves under
- "The Eternal Fire of Love and Devotion" to keep them warm from the inside out

As they looked closer, they realized the parchment showed the different stages and changes the jungle would go through, the places they would visit, and even details about challenges they'd face in the future. It included specific strategies to increase their effectiveness and success on these challenges. It was so simple and clear that it almost felt like "cheating."

> WE MAY FEEL AS THOUGH WE'VE BEEN DUMPED IN THE MIDDLE OF AN UNFAMILIAR AND DANGEROUS JUNGLE.

With this map, they not only understood their jungle and how it would sustain them through the years, they also knew better what to expect and how to get through the challenges so their team came out winners.

Wow! They realized all the supplies and information they needed for themselves and their children to survive—and even to thrive—in this jungle for the next several years were indicated right here on this little piece of parchment. They just needed the map, the instructions, to tap into their jungle's true potential. They knew they'd chosen the right box and the treasure inside would help their marriage survive the parenting jungle and help grow their children into the strongest, healthiest adults possible. Their fears quickly faded; they held in their hands a true treasure.

YOUR PERSONAL TREASURE MAP

Parenting often feels like the ultimate survival challenge—a place where unexpected "traps" seem to loom large and fearfully in the brush. Like Matt and Laura, we may feel as though we've been dumped in the middle of an unfamiliar and dangerous jungle with absolutely no equipment or instructions, and we're expected to survive for the next eighteen years. We flounder around trying to make do with what we have, constantly searching for something—anything—to give direction and aid. But the jungle seems to be growing too fast for us to keep up, and before long we realize we're losing this game of "survival of the fittest."

We parents who desperately search for aid to escape the traps in today's parenting jungle are presented with a large array of theories, opinions, statistics, and "perfect-world" suggestions. Yet sometimes when we try to use these to conquer our real-world challenges, we seem to fall flat and end up right back where we started. It's like being out in the parenting jungle, opening a large crate marked "Parents' Treasure Box: all the supplies a good parent needs," and finding roller skates, a basketball, and the latest electronic game—not at all what you needed or hoped for. Yet many parents today are settling for that box of "supplies" and trying to parent with just a bunch of toys.

THE TRUE TREASURE OF PARENTING IS FOUND MORE IN THE RELATIONSHIPS THAN THE RULES.

This book is what we parents are really searching for. It's a true treasure chest, the ultimate parents' survival kit, full of practical parenting techniques that are simple to implement yet extremely effective. This back-to-basics book, firmly grounded in sound biblical principles, will give desperate and thirsty parents a long, cool drink of suggestions that really work with children of all ages.

You'll learn the basics of discipline, communication, and growing responsible adults, but parenting is much more than getting your child to do what you want him or her to do. Although sections of the book are full of specific skills, if you picked it up looking for a new way to change your child's behavior, you may be disappointed. The true treasure of parenting is found more in the relationships than the rules. This book is about seeing your children as the treasure and blessing they are and taking on your full, God-given responsibility to help them grow in wisdom, stature, and favor with God and man. It's about demonstrating unconditional love and acceptance and training them up in the way they should go, to be everything God created them to be. It's about loving them into adulthood.

You're about to begin searching the treasure map that will help you maneuver and survive the traps of the parenting jungle. As you do, I want to clarify a couple of things. First, for ease of reading I've chosen to describe your child as either masculine or feminine in alternating chapters. Second, at the end of each chapter I've included a "Parenting in Practice" suggestion that I hope will help move you to action. Some of these relate directly to the chapter; others may be more general parenting tips or suggestions. However, all are designed to move you out of the book and into a stronger relationship with your child.

GOD HAS PROVIDED US WITH WONDERFUL GUIDELINES TO GET US THROUGH.

So now, as you begin your journey to better parenting, I encourage you to embrace this book and the privilege of parenting with wide-open arms and mind. The information and suggestions here are so simple, clear, and effective you just might feel like you're "cheating" as you maneuver past the "traps" of parenting challenges with more ease and success than you ever thought possible.

CHAPTER 1

TRAIN UP A CHILD

The Basics of Healthy Parenting

A little boy was overheard praying one night, "Dear God, please take care of my daddy and my mommy and my sister and my bother and my doggy. Oh, and please take care of yourself, God. If anything happens to you, we're gonna be in a big mess."

How true that is. Without God in the picture, leading and guiding us every step of the way, we'd really be in a big mess, especially when it comes to trying to raise our children. But luckily God didn't give us this job of parenting and then check out and leave us to our own devices to figure it all out. He may not have taped instruction manuals to their backsides, but God has provided us with wonderful guidelines to get us through this most challenging task.

First, he teaches us through his relationship with us. Through his interactions with us, he models how to be the best parent possible. As parents, it's our job to study and learn from his example. Second, he teaches us about parenting through his direct instructions in Scripture. By reading the Bible, we know we are to model to our children, discipline

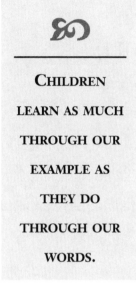

CHILDREN LEARN AS MUCH THROUGH OUR EXAMPLE AS THEY DO THROUGH OUR WORDS.

them, and teach them to fear the Lord and obey his commandments. Our own relationship with the Father and the instructions he has given us teach us how to show unconditional love, strengthen and encourage our children, respond appropriately to sin and disobedience, and demonstrate effective discipline in our relationships with our children. In this chapter, we'll explore what our biblical responsibility as parents actually is and how to go about raising our children in a God-honoring way.

TWO SIDES OF THE SAME COIN

As we look at Scripture to determine exactly what we're supposed to do with these little bundles of joy, we quickly learn we're instructed to do two main things. Deuteronomy 6:6–9 shows both: "These commandments that I give you today are to be upon your hearts. Impress them on your children. Talk about them when you sit at home and when you walk along the road, when you lie down and when you get up." We're to "impress" our children and "talk" to them. So what does that really mean?

"Impress them" refers mainly to what we'd call "hands-on training." It's learning that occurs through experience. The other side of the parenting coin is "talking." This is teaching through our words. For parenting to be effective, both must be present. Neither words nor actions alone are sufficient.

If we're going to be effective parents, we need to understand both training and teaching.

Train Them

Training is the part of parenting that involves a hands-on approach. These are the things we instill in our children through action (theirs and ours). Children learn as much (if not more) through our example as they do through our words. As a matter of fact, they begin following our example long before they can even understand our words. Infants can mimic behaviors they see done over and over, such as wave bye-bye, blow kisses, and smile—even though they don't comprehend language. One of the very first ways we begin to teach our children is through modeling for them.

Early on, a child mimicking our behaviors is encouraged and praised. We seem to be telling him "do what I do" and are thrilled when he actually does. But what about later on? As your child grows and has developed past the stage of "bye-bye," dressing himself, and proper table manners, do you still look on his imitation of you as "cute"? As children grow and develop, they move away from copying our body movements to reproducing our character traits and social interactions (unfortunately, usually about the time Grandma or the pastor is visiting).

Effective child-training requires you to be shamelessly aware of what your behaviors are saying, and doing your very best to make your actions measure up to the instructions in God's Word. God directs us to be a model to our children. "These are the commands, decrees and laws the Lord your God directed me to teach you to observe ... so that you, your children and their children after them may fear the Lord your God as long as you live" (Deut. 6:1–2). As we look closely at this passage, we see we're directed first and foremost to obey these commands ourselves. God told Moses to instruct the parents to *observe* his commands "so that" the children would fear the Lord. It didn't say to "teach" the children to fear the Lord (although we know from later verses that's part of it). It tells the parents to do what the commandments say. Our children learn what the commandments are through what we do, not through our speaking them in words. Kids know a hypocrite when they see one and will grow to have no respect for such a person.

God knew the power of modeling. If the parents obey the commands, their children learn to do the same by watching. You can't teach your children by telling them to do something they've never seen you implement in your own life.

TEACH THEM

"These commandments that I give you today are to be upon your hearts. Impress them on your children. Talk about them when you sit at home and when you walk along the road, when you lie down and when you get up" (Deut. 6:6–9). The second side of the parenting coin is teaching. Teaching refers mainly to the words that we use to teach and guide our children. But here, Scripture tells us that what we plan to teach our children should "be upon your hearts" first. If we are to teach God's commands, we must first know them ourselves. As parents, we're to think on them often, study them, and memorize them so that wherever we are, we have the knowledge available to us to impart it to our children. Just as you can't teach something you don't *live*, you can't teach or live something you don't *know*.

HOW TO SUCCEED IN TEACHING AND TRAINING

To adequately teach and train our children, we must do three things:

Be intentional. Effective parenting doesn't just happen. It requires that we seize every opportunity we possibly can to train our children in the "way he should go." Being intentional involves planning and setting time aside for formal teaching between parent and child. But that's not all it means.

If we simply wait for the right moment or until we have time to sit down and officially instruct, we'll miss many real-life opportunities to train our kids. Being intentional also means always being on the lookout for "life lessons"—opportunities that spontaneously occur in daily life. If we aren't actively watching for these chances to teach, they'll quickly pass us by.

THE PROBLEM IS NOT THE NUMBER OF HOURS AVAILABLE, BUT HOW WE CHOOSE TO FILL THEM.

Be available. You can't teach and train your children if you don't spend time with them. How do you expect to talk to them "when you sit at home and when you walk along the road, when you lie down and when you get up," if you're not with them at home, on the road, at night, and in the morning? One of today's biggest parenting challenges is we just don't seem to have enough time. But last time I checked, our days are no shorter than those of generations past. We have the same number of hours in our day that the people in Moses' time did. The problem is not the number of hours available, but how we choose to fill them. To be effective, we must understand that parenting is a 24-hours-a-day, 7-days-a-week, 365-days-a-year job. We must make ourselves available to our children if we ever hope to fulfill what God requires of us.

Be flexible. Effective parents understand that each child is different, with different personalities and temperaments, talents and skills, fears and concerns, energy levels, needs, thoughts and feelings, and different styles of interacting with the world around them. Helping a child grow, develop, and reach his fullest potential means being flexible with how you teach and train. "Train [up] a child in the way *he* should go" (Prov. 22:6) indicates that each child's training should be unique. There's no room here for "cookie-cutter" parenting that assumes each child will respond the same as his peers. That's simply not the case and will do our children a great disservice. The instruction we give our children should be individual and directed toward that child's unique talents, personality, and temperament.

> **THEY NEED PRACTICE TO DEVELOP THE SKILLS THEY'RE TRYING TO LEARN.**

The verse doesn't say train up a child in the way ...

"you want him to go."

"his brothers and sisters should go."

"others will go."

It says in the way *he* should go. Personalizing our parenting to each child individually will require us to rely even more on God's loving guidance and wisdom, because only *he* knows where that particular child's path is leading.

WHY MUST WE "TEACH" AND "TRAIN"?

Our job as parents is to raise our children to be responsible adults capable of functioning appropriately in the world around them. Children aren't born knowing right from wrong. If they don't learn it at home, where do you think they'll learn it? I sure don't want this world to be teaching its view of right and wrong to my kids. The family unit is the basic social unit and should be the primary source of learning for children.

It's in the home that children first learn to love, play, share, and cooperate. There they learn how to treat others and how they can expect others to treat them. In the home, children build the foundation of who they are and what they believe. Our children will then take all they've learned with them as they leave the home and venture out into the world.

Children have so many lessons and skills to learn that they must start early to master as many as possible before leaving the nest. But what if a child grows up in a home where his parents choose not to teach and train him? What if his parents focus mainly on protecting him from the world's cold, cruel realities in hopes of helping him avoid the pain the world can bring? Although their intentions may be good, parents who avoid the teaching and training every child needs will definitely *not* produce a responsible and functional adult capable of making healthy choices for himself.

IT'S OK TO LET THEM FALL

If you want your kids to be able to make good choices as teens and young adults, then they have to learn how. They need practice to develop the skills they're trying to learn. Giving them this practice early in life helps the falls not hurt as much.

Consider a child learning to walk. Since we know he won't master this skill on his first attempt, we stand close by, watching and encouraging his efforts. We're within reach if he panics and can quickly grab a hand when he's headed to the floor. The more assured he becomes, the farther Mom and Dad back up (a little at a time). Eventually, we're no longer within arm's length.

As the child continues practicing, the risk of pain is

somewhat greater but still not severe. When the toddler loses his balance, he has only a little way to fall and has plenty of padding around the place most likely to hit the floor. Most of all, Mom and Dad are still right there to offer hugs, comfort, and encouragement to try again. And as he continues to try over and over, he begins to master the steps, maintain his balance, and move about his world with a newfound sense of security and confidence. These skills will continue to develop until he is ready to run toward his future, steady and confident.

But what if this baby is carried all the time? He's never allowed to try out his legs because his parents are afraid he'll fall and get hurt, so they keep him off the ground and in their arms for as long as they possibly can. They may tell him that someday he'll need to learn to walk on his own two feet and may even instruct him verbally on how to do that. But he's never allowed to practice while he's little and it's safe. Eventually he's so big the parents simply can't hold him any-more and must release him. As they put him down, what do you think will happen?

That child may be paralyzed and completely unable to move around his world and take care of himself. Or he may have just enough strength in his legs and determination in his soul to push himself up and try to balance. As he takes his first step, he begins to waver. As this massive boy/man sways out of control, he realizes the floor is a long way down and looks very hard.

The parents stand by wondering what to do and realize they have only two choices. They can jump in and try to rescue their falling child, only to be taken down with him and smashed beneath the weight of the fall. Or they can stand by and watch exactly what they'd been hoping to avoid by carry-ing him all these years. He's going to get hurt, and there's very little they can do about it now. The time to teach and intervene with minimal pain has long since passed. He's being sent into the world unsteady, weak, and insecure.

It may seem ridiculous to consider parents never letting a child walk because they're afraid he'll fall, but many parents are overprotecting their children in the name of love. Of course we're to shield our kids from the world's evils and from major harm. But caring for and loving your kids doesn't mean protecting them from all pain or danger. It doesn't mean we should make things "easier" for them by doing it for them hoping to help them avoid any frustration. We should protect but not overprotect. We should have authority but not unhealthy control.

OUR KIDS NEED US TO BE PARENTS, NOT FRIENDS.

I heard a story about a man who came across a butterfly cocoon with a very small opening in it. As he stopped and watched, the butterfly began to emerge. For several hours, it struggled to force its body through this tiny hole and eventually seemed to give up. It seemed to have gone as far as it could and was now stuck half in and half out. The man felt sorry for the butterfly and decided to help it out. He took a pair of scissors and cut the cocoon open and freed the butterfly. But as the butterfly emerged, it appeared deformed. Its body was fat and swollen, its wings were shriveled, and it was completely incapable of flying.

It wasn't until later that the man learned why this butterfly could never fly. The restricting cocoon and the intense struggle to emerge through that tiny opening were actually necessary for the butterfly's future ability to fly. Through the process of squeezing out of the cocoon, the fluid from a butterfly's body is forced into its wings so they'll be big and strong enough to fly once released.

Sometimes life's struggles and the pain associated with them are needed to strengthen us and our children to manage life's trials. If we remove these obstacles from our children's lives because we don't want to watch them struggle through the pain, we just might cripple them and keep them from being strong and ready to fly.

SCRIMMAGE TIME

As parents, we need to accept and perform our God-given authority over our homes. Our kids need us to be parents, not friends. You can enjoy your time together, but our role is so much more. We're not here simply as cheerleaders (although cheering them on in their good choices is part of parenting); we also must be their coaches.

> HELPING CHILDREN LEARN TO MAKE CHOICES EARLY IN LIFE IS MUCH SAFER.

A good football coach doesn't just have his players sit in the locker room talking and reading about the game and the plays necessary to win. He doesn't keep them on the bench simply watching others play, hoping they'll learn by example. He also doesn't just take his players out on the field and tell them to "go at it," hoping they'll instinctively know how to play. Any of these teaching techniques would leave the players unprepared.

Good coaching includes verbal teaching, then letting them try out what they learned. The coach understands that practicing the techniques is part of learning, but the real test is the scrimmage. This is a "safe" environment that lets players practice their new skills in a simulated game. The plays are real, but the consequences of a win or loss aren't all that painful. The actual season hasn't started. Although the hits and falls still hurt, they're buffered by the realization that this doesn't go on the record. It's just practice; the goal is to perfect the skill. When mistakes are made, both coaches and players know there's still time to make adjustments on how to best handle that situation in the real game. As players succeed on the scrimmage field, their confidence builds, and the pride of a job well done helps spur them on to future successes.

Coaches who decide not to scrimmage because the players might get hurt aren't preparing them for the real game. A player from this type of team will be thrown into the game of life unprepared, weak, and insecure. His first big blow from someone headed in the opposite direction will likely knock the wind completely out of him or, worse, render him completely helpless. His head will be spinning both from the blow and from the realization that this can be a cruel game and no one out there intends to pamper him. He thought the rules didn't apply to him. He expected to continue to be the center of the universe. He was sure that when he wanted to go one way and call his own shots, everyone else would be thrilled and make sure there was nothing and no one in his path that could cause him pain. But reality will soon set in, and the hits will come hard and fast. Then all the coach can do is stand on the sideline and pray that the damage isn't life-threatening.

How Big Will Their First Choice Be?

Helping children learn to make choices early in life, when the wrong choice may hurt only a little, is much safer for everyone involved. None of us likes to see our children hurt, but the pain of leaving a homework assignment at home and getting an F because Mom and Dad wouldn't "fix" the problem is much less painful than losing a job because the child never learned responsibility.

If we help our children learn to make healthy choices while they're still young and safe at home, they'll be much more prepared to face the world. But if we insist on making all the decisions ourselves "because we know best" and refuse to let our children experience the consequences of their actions and choices, we've robbed our children of valuable lessons. You could send your child out into the world floundering, and the first choice he has to make could be a major, life-or-death kind of decision. Are you willing to accept those consequences? Well, I'm not! And if you aren't either, you must give your children practice at making their own choices as they grow. Stop making their choices for them and stop rescuing them from the consequences of their actions.

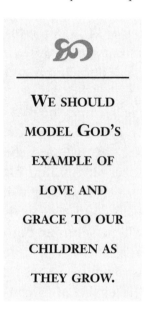

WE SHOULD MODEL GOD'S EXAMPLE OF LOVE AND GRACE TO OUR CHILDREN AS THEY GROW.

Even God gives his children the right to make their own choices ... and the freedom to experience the consequences of those choices. Of course, he desires that we'll choose rightly, and he's willing to share his wisdom with us and guide us when we ask. But, he's also willing to let us screw it all up if that's what we are determined to do. He knows we can learn from our mistakes and in doing so can grow closer to him. He forgives us and is always willing to give us another chance. We should model his example of love and grace to our children as they grow. "Effective parenting centers around love—love that is not permissive, love that doesn't tolerate disrespect, but also love that is powerful enough to allow kids to make mistakes and permit them to live with the consequences of those mistakes."[1]

PARENTING IN PRACTICE

Here's your very first "homework" (that's what I call these suggestions in my office) to help you get out of the pages of this book and into a growing relationship with your children.

DREAM GOD'S DREAMS FOR YOUR CHILD

We all have big dreams for our kids. But it really doesn't matter if they live up to our dreams. As a matter of fact, sometimes that can simply put pressure on them to "live up to what Mom and Dad want me to be." But what does matter is that they become what God has intended them to become. Dreaming God's dreams for your children means praying for them to reach their God-given potential and letting them know that you do. Here are a couple of ways you can communicate that you're dreaming God's dreams for them. First, pray with them, for them, and over them often. As you do, ask God to reveal his plan for your child and help you do all you can to help your child reach that potential. Second, write a letter of blessing to your child, putting on paper what you hope and pray for his life. Remember, this is not about your expectations. Instead, it's about growing him closer to God.

CHAPTER 2

AND THE TWO SHALL BE ONE

Being a Good Parenting Team

 Think about a time when you were embarking on something new—maybe something you'd dreamed about and looked forward to for years. How did you feel as the event drew closer? You likely had feelings of excitement and positive anticipation mixed with fear and anxiety over the unknown. Or consider a time when you had a challenge or problem that seemed insurmountable; you probably felt inadequate and helpless. Both these types of events likely caused you to seek out others for their help and support. Humans are social creatures and generally tend to look for other humans to share their experiences in both positive and negative circumstances.

I've heard it said that marriage and friendship "divide the pain and multiply the joy" of our experiences. Going it alone not only leaves us to struggle alone, it also robs us of sharing the joys.

We weren't intended to face the challenges and responsibilities of parenting alone. The family was created to include a husband and wife raising their children together. I'm sure

God knew just how hard parenting was going to be, and that's why he set it up to be managed by a team, not an individual. The husband and wife each have unique talents, skills, and perspectives that, blended together, provide for the children's needs in the healthiest and most balanced way. This team approach also offers support and encouragement for the parents themselves. We're less likely to burn out when we have someone fighting the battles with us and letting us "tag team" it at times.

WE NEED TO LOVE OURSELVES AND TEACH OUR CHILDREN TO LOVE THEMSELVES AS WELL.

Of course, this is the best-case scenario, where a husband and wife are living and raising their children together. But this isn't the case for the majority of the United States today. The increase in divorce and remarriage has redefined the family unit, but the concepts of parenting and working together as a team can and should still be applied. Children benefit when their parents get along and work together to raise them, whether or not they live in the same house (although it's usually easier that way). These concepts can also apply to stepfamily situations. The ultimate goal is to be the best parents you can be to raise the healthiest children you can.

The first concern isn't the skills you may learn, but whether or not you have what it takes to be a good parenting team. Three specific things determine which teams will perform best in this challenge: the emotional health of each of your individual members, the health of your marital relationship, and your ability to work well together as a team.

This chapter will examine the most significant skills needed to keep your "team" strong while you're working to raise your children. (If you'd like more information on this topic, my book *Childproofing Your Marriage: Keeping Your Marriage a Priority During the Parenting Years* is specifically devoted to that.) Here we'll take time to discuss having a healthy self-esteem, putting the marriage first, and co-parenting.

HEALTHY SELF-ESTEEM

You want a child who grows up exhibiting a strong and healthy view of herself, right? Well, how do you expect her to learn to have good self-esteem? Do you think she'll simply look in the mirror one day and say, "Wow! I really like who I am"? If that's what you're hoping for, you'll be sadly disappointed.

Our children need help in learning to like and love themselves just the way they are, and one of the most effective ways they learn is through their eyes. They watch everything and model much of what they see—including self-concept. Parents with low self-esteem likely will have kids with low self-esteem.

The Bible says, "Love your neighbor *as* yourself" (Matt. 22:39). That means we need to love ourselves and teach our children to love themselves as well. If we're always putting ourselves last and putting ourselves down, our kids will learn to do the same.

Not long ago, I saw this play out in one particular family. I was treating a woman who was seriously struggling with her own personal self-esteem issues. She was successful in her job and well liked by her friends, family, and coworkers, but none of that seemed to

> ONE OF THE FIRST STEPS IN BEING A GOOD PARENT IS BELIEVING YOU'RE A GOOD PERSON.

matter to her. She felt ugly, fat, unworthy, and useless in almost every area of her life. We worked for several months on helping her see herself as God sees her. She learned to identify the negative things she'd been saying to herself for years and began to change those old tapes.

From this new vantage point, she noticed her eleven-year-old son was seriously struggling with low self-esteem. Before she worked on herself, she had difficulty seeing this, but now she sat in my office crying, "Did I teach him that?" Unfortunately, the answer was, "At least in part, yes." Her young son was saying many of the same negative things about himself that she not so long ago had been saying. She hadn't realized the impact of her own self-esteem on those around her because she had been so wrapped up in herself. She thought she had hid it well, put on a great mask, and acted like all the other moms. But now she realized her mask wasn't as good as she thought. Because she hadn't liked herself, she seemed unable to teach her son he should and could like himself. Because she didn't really believe she was valuable to God or anyone else, neither did her son.

We all want our kids to grow up knowing they're special, unique, and wonderful. We want them to feel loved and lovable, valuable and worthy, and grow up confident and secure. But you can't give your child something you don't possess yourself. So, one of the first steps in being a good parent is believing you're a good person.

Don't you know that God sees us as his greatest creation? Well, look back in the first chapter of Genesis at the week of creation. At the end of each day, God looked at what he had made and evaluated it:

- After making the land and sea, he said it was good (v. 10).
- After making the plants, he said it was good (v. 12).

- After making the sun, moon, and stars, he said it was good (v. 18).
- After making the fish and birds, he said it was good (v. 21).
- After making the animals, he said it was good (v. 25).

Then, on the sixth day, God created man. At the end of that day, when God evaluated his work, do you know what he said?

- He said it was very good (v. 31)!

When you look at yourself, do you like what you see? God does. He loves you and wants you to know that you're valuable. Like any good father, God wants his children to like themselves and have a healthy self-esteem.

I believe Jesus modeled healthy self-esteem while he was here on earth—not inflated (even though he was God) and not degraded. He knew how to care for himself, be true to himself and his convictions, assert himself when necessary, and let others know who he was in an appropriate way. He never talked down about himself or his achievements. I don't think he ever performed a miracle and then said, "That really wasn't good enough. I should do better next time."

How about you? Can you look in the mirror and tell yourself you're a good person? Can you make a list of things you like about yourself? Can you model healthy self-esteem for your children? If not, make it a priority to work on improving your own attitude. This will help you, your marriage, and your children.

PUTTING THE MARRIAGE FIRST

If you're married, either to your child's biological or stepparent, you must learn to make your marital relationship a priority.

Children need to feel secure in their home environment, and a strong and growing marriage helps establish that sense of security. When the adults in the home are always in conflict or simply coexist, children may feel the ground under their feet is shaky. Also, when couples put all their attention and energy into the children at the expense of their marriage, children get the message that they're the center of the universe and everything revolves around them.

IF YOU TRULY WANT A THRIVING MARITAL GARDEN, YOU'LL HAVE TO GIVE IT REGULAR ATTENTION.

So for the marriage and the children's sake, please keep your marriage one of your very highest priorities. This means more than a quick kiss in the morning or a hug and a "hi" in the evening as you pass each other on your way to different children's activities.

Marriage is much like a garden we cultivate and plant during the important dating stage. But the problem arises when, after the wedding, we stop attending to the garden and get busy with other activities. We don't have much time, so we run by, check on the garden, water it a little, and go on our way. When we return months or even years later, we find a jungle of weeds choking out whatever was originally planted there.

Unfortunately, that's what happens to many couples, especially those trying to raise children. If you truly want a thriving marital garden, you'll have to give it regular attention. If you realize you've let your garden become overgrown, you may have some hard work ahead of you. But once you take the time and energy to get the garden back in shape, the daily investment to keep it healthy and growing is much less.

A couple who had been married several years was smack-dab in the middle of the parenting jungle. They hadn't been on a date in ages, but hadn't really realized how far they had let things slip. Then one Saturday morning, while the wife was washing dishes, her husband walked up behind her and asked, "Would you like to go out, girl?"

Without even turning around, the wife quickly responded with a thrilled, "Yes, I'd love to!" They had a wonderful evening together and it wasn't until the end of the date that the husband made his confession. Smiling, he told his wife that the question he'd asked that morning had actually been directed to the family dog lying on the kitchen floor. They had a great laugh while realizing something needed to change.

> HEALTHY COUPLES DON'T "FIND" TIME TO BE TOGETHER, THEY "MAKE" IT.

Making your marriage a priority will mean devoting time to be together. That seemed to come easy (or at least easier) during dating and the early years of marriage. Why is it so hard now? Yes, we have more responsibilities now, such as children, consuming our lives. But the primary difference is the effort and importance we give it. If we really want to do something, we can find the time.

I know your life is filled with important things and the challenge is finding the right balance. But if you're always pushing your spouse aside to spend time with the kids, consider what you're teaching them. Are you modeling how they should treat their future husbands or wives? Probably not. Spending time with your spouse not only draws the two of you closer—it also teaches your children that marriage has to be our number one human relationship. Although they sometimes may complain when you take "mommy and daddy" time, they quickly learn their home is happier, safer, and more secure when you do.

Starting right now, show your spouse your marriage is a priority by taking time to be together. You may have a list of excuses why you can't seem to find the time, but healthy couples don't "find" time to be together, they "make" it. You have time to do whatever you most want to do. If you don't spend the time with your spouse, you'll simply fill it with something less important. Here are a few suggestions to get you started:

CREATING QUALITY TIME TOGETHER

1. Hire a sitter and get away from the house for a real, old-fashioned date. Try to have a date night at least once a week.

2. Learn to date at home. Create special time at home for just the two of you when you can't get a sitter or afford to go out.

3. Avoid overcommitting. Be selective about what outside events and responsibilities you commit to. Be sure to check with your spouse before signing on.

4. Set aside daily "mommy and daddy" time. Even fifteen to twenty minutes a day can help you stay connected. Taking this time daily helps your children learn to respect your couple time and models to them how important you are to each other.

5. Learn about your spouse's interests so you can do them together. When I started taking an interest in football, Jim was thrilled. Now we hardly ever miss a game.

6. Read or watch the news together. Share your thoughts and feelings about what's going on in the world.

7. Share a cup of coffee together before the kids wake up or a beverage after they go to bed.

8. Go on a walk together. Consider having the older kids watch the younger ones and take a walkie-talkie with you.

9. Put a lock on your bedroom door and use it.

10. Send the kids to bed early. They need more rest than you may realize and you need the quality time together.

CO-PARENTING

Another tool you'll need in your survival arsenal is the ability to co-parent. Whether you have a nuclear, divorced, or blended family, the parents' ability to work together for the child's sake is paramount in her overall development.

Parents often tell me they feel alone even when the other parent is around and active in the child's life. One of the biggest complaints is that one parent (in the home or not) seems uninterested and uninvolved in the parenting process, leaving all or most of the work to the other. A woman may say she feels like she has one extra kid in the house when her husband is there and she has to "parent" him right along with the children. Or a man may complain that his wife refuses to discipline the children, always making him the "bad guy." Parenting alone when you shouldn't have to is frustrating and tiring, and also sends poor messages to your children.

> TO AVOID THESE PROBLEMS, YOU'LL NEED TO LEARN AND IMPLEMENT CO-PARENTING.

As bad as this is, the second common complaint is even more destructive—one parent undermining and sabotaging the other's efforts. When Mom sets a "no snacks before dinner" rule, then Dad slips Junior a couple of cookies to hold him over, the parenting team has been compromised. When Dad grounds Sis for two weeks, and Mom thinks the punishment is too harsh and drops it after one week, the fracture in the parenting team widens. Unfortunately, when parents aren't co-parenting, such situations are likely to occur over and over. Each time they do, both children and adults are affected negatively. The kids learn to play one parent against the other to manipulate the system in their favor. The adults' relationship is pushed to the limits. They begin to feel the enemy has invaded their camp. The home's safety and security is in jeopardy, and the parent's conflicts will eventually drive a wedge between them.

To avoid these problems, you'll need to learn and implement "co-parenting"—cooperating in all areas of parenting. This means doing things together and accepting that you're both equally responsible for raising your children. Co-parents work together to set family rules and consequences, decide on family responsibilities, and manage the home's daily needs. Anything that involves parenting involves both parents.

WHENEVER POSSIBLE, CO-PARENTS TRY TO MAKE THEIR DISCIPLINE DECISIONS TOGETHER.

The co-parenting concept has grown over the last few decades in tandem with the increasing number of dual-income families. With both parents working outside the home, the requirements of running the household have started to be more evenly divided. More fathers are participating in responsibilities such as cooking, cleaning, laundry, and childcare. But even in families where one parent (not always the mom anymore) works at home while the other works outside the home—or if the biological parents live in different homes—learning to cooperate in the parenting process is beneficial.

Co-parenting is especially important in discipline. Taking time to discuss in advance what views each of you have on discipline can help tremendously. You need to decide together what techniques you plan to use, what rules you need to establish, and what the consequences will be for noncompliance. You need to be on the same page if you're going to parent and discipline your children as a team.

EVEN IF YOU DON'T AGREE ON HOW THE SITUATION WAS HANDLED, SUPPORT YOUR SPOUSE IN FRONT OF YOUR CHILD.

Whenever possible, co-parents try to make their discipline decisions together. Still, one parent often will have to make an on-the-spot decision. Although your basic, agreed-upon guidelines will help, that's no guarantee that you'll choose the action your spouse would have chosen in your place. Disagreements are bound to occur. How you handle these disagreements tells both you and your children how united the two of you really are.

Here are some ways you can keep your team strong:

Don't argue about parenting and discipline decisions in front of the children. This applies whether you're working together to come up with an appropriate discipline or if one of you had to make a decision without the other. Any disagreement about the best decision should stay behind closed doors. During that private time, devise a solution both of you can agree on. That way, when you return to your child you will be able to present a "we" instead of an "I" decision.

Support the decisions your spouse makes. If you are gone for the afternoon and come home to find your spouse grounded your daughter from the computer for two weeks for what seems to you a minor offense, don't say, "Two weeks? You have to be kidding!" All that does is undermine your spouse's authority and show your daughter there's a weak link in the parenting team. Even if you don't agree on how the situation was handled, support your spouse in front of your child. You may want to talk about it privately later. As you do, take time to hear the whole story and your spouse's reasons for the decision he or she made. You may realize you didn't know the whole story and can now better understand the outcome.

If you still don't agree with your spouse, you have two choices. First, decide if this is a battle worth fighting. Will the world end if you support and follow through with the decision? Probably not. So, unless the situation is going to cause long-term damage, seriously consider supporting it.

The second option is to openly express to your spouse why you disagree and work toward a compromise. Once you have agreed on a resolution, present it to your child as a team. Let her know the two of you discussed this and have decided together to overturn the previous decision.

Don't let your kids play you against each other. "Mom said I could play next door with Megan." "Dad told me it was OK to listen to that CD." Sound familiar? We've all experienced the "Mom said Dad said" strategy from our children (and tried it ourselves when we were young). This obvious "divide and conquer" technique can cause considerable damage to the parenting team if we aren't prepared for it. If you fall into the trap of simply believing the other parent actually did say whatever your child claims, you may find yourself arguing with your spouse before you verify it. "I can't believe you told Sarah she could listen to that CD. You know we agreed to no hard rock." And before your spouse can confirm or deny saying that, you two are off and running (and Sarah is listening to her CD).

Another way this strategy plays out is when your child asks one of you if she can do something. If she doesn't like the response, she asks the other parent. Without knowing your spouse already said no, you may say yes. Having gotten the "right" answer, your child gleefully goes about doing whatever at least one of you told her not to do. Again, this not only shows your children that your team isn't unified, it also likely will cause more parental conflicts.

The best defense against this strategy is a simple: "Let's go check with your mom (or dad) about this." Once your children know you'll check in with each other and make decisions together, you'll have rendered this technique useless.

Parenting in Practice

You Are My Sunshine List

This exercise will help you enhance your child's self-esteem. Make a separate list for each child of the positive traits you see in her. List all those things you really like about her. You even may want to put it in the form of a love letter.

This will do two things: First, it will cause you to keep your thoughts about your children positive. Second, when you share it with your child, you will make her feel great. At the end, your child will have a list of all the things you like about her to read as often as she chooses.

CHAPTER 3

YOU ARE MY SUNSHINE

Learning to TREASURE Your Child

A couple is walking along the road when they happen on an unusual little man who offers them the opportunity of a lifetime. In his say-it-as-fast-as-you-can manner, he tells them he knows about a "treasure" they could get their hands on if they're interested. He explains, "Of course, the opportunity to get this treasure will cost you a bit, but it's worth every penny." They look at each other and shake their heads in disbelief, realizing he's obviously a salesman and possibly a con artist, and begin to walk away. But their curiosity gets the best of them, and they come back to find out what kind of treasure this guy has to offer.

As he works to reel them in, he explains the treasure he knows about would be a wonderful addition to any home. It would be so awe-inspiring they simply wouldn't be able to take their eyes off it once they had one of their very own. "Once you get one of these treasures, your life will never be the same, and you will wonder how you ever lived without it," the little man explains. The couple can't wait to find out what this amazing treasure could be and, of course, how much it costs. They wonder if they would be willing to pay.

Finally, the little man exposes his secret, "The treasure I'm talking about is called ... a child." Surprised, the couple ponders the idea that a child actually could be considered a "treasure." They challenge the little man with things they've heard about raising children.

> **LEARNING TO FOCUS ON THE TREASURE IN OUR CHILDREN WILL HELP US AVOID MISSING OUT ON THE MANY BLESSINGS GOD HAS IN STORE.**

"How can you consider something that is estimated to cost close to $200,000 from birth to age eighteen a treasure?" the husband asks.

"Well, I did tell you that it would cost a bit."

"And surely you wouldn't expect us to be dumb enough to pay that kind of money for something that will keep us up at night, steal practically all our energy and time, throw up on us, argue with us, embarrass us in the grocery store, and cause us endless amounts of worry and stress, do you?" the wife practically yells.

The little man explains, "Yes, I agree that's a lot of money for something that can be difficult at times. But have you considered everything you're getting for that price? For mere dollars a day, you'll get: exclusive naming rights, smiles that melt your heart, giggles under the covers, and butterfly kisses. This deal will grant you the right to never completely grow up, as you'll need to be available for finger painting, Saturday-morning cartoons, and chasing lightning bugs. This investment will pay off an amazingly high rate of return through dividends of snuggles, birthday wishes, refrigerator art, and memories that last a lifetime. Now, is any amount of money too much to pay for a true treasure like that?"

The couple realizes they'd completely missed the point and would have missed the blessing if they focused only on what a child would cost them. Now they had a new perspective. The blessings a child would bring into their world would far outweigh their monetary investment. This truly was a priceless treasure.

It really is a matter of perspective. Learning to focus on the treasure in our children will help us avoid missing out on the many blessings God has in store for us as we parent. We'll be better able to help them believe in themselves and grow to be everything God intended them to be.

So, how do you learn to treasure your child? Let's break treasuring down into its components and discuss each one in detail.

T   Take time
R   Reach out
E   Encourage
A   Accept
S   Shield
U   Understand
R   Respect
E   Establish boundaries

T—Take Time

I waited while you spoke,
I listened to your reasoning;
while you were searching for words,
I gave you my full attention.

—Job 32:11–12

More than almost anything else, children need our time. The problem is, in our society time seems to be in low supply. If we aren't careful, the activities we believe we "have to" and "should" do eat up all our time, and our children are the ones who pay. We may try to relieve our guilt by rationalizing that all these activities are for our child. We're just trying to give him all the opportunities we never had, right? But truthfully, our kids don't need these activities nearly as much as they need quality time with us.

WHEN YOUR WORDS AND ACTIONS MATCH, YOUR CHILD WILL TRULY FEEL TREASURED.

Besides, are we really signing little Brent up for all these wonderful experiences for his own sake, or just dragging him to practice when he'd rather stay home? Our society seems to tell us that if we don't get our child involved (or overinvolved), we're bad parents. If you're keeping Brent busy so you won't look like a deadbeat parent who doesn't care enough to get her kid involved, you may want to reevaluate your motives.

We also may try to relieve our guilt through "flooding." Flooding seems to occur most in dual-income homes where both parents are over-committed to work and personal demands. Eventually, the guilt of running one hundred miles per hour and barely seeing your kids takes over and you try to make up for lost time, trying to cram as much "quality" time as possible into a few extended periods throughout the year. We tell our kids we don't have time to play right now but just wait until we go on vacation.

Your child doesn't care about what's going to happen in a couple of months—he just wants time with you today. Taking time for your child will require adjusting your schedule to be at his activities, teaching him to do things around the house (even when you know you could do it quicker alone), and reducing the number of outside activities to allow more family time. (More about "quality" time in chapter 4.)

R—Reach Out to Them

And he [Jesus] took the children in his arms,
put his hands on them and blessed them.

—Mark 10:16

Reaching out to your child includes any and all ways you can show you love him. It means putting your money where your mouth is and making your actions match your words. Telling your child you love him with your mouth is important, but telling him you love him with your actions seals the deal. When your words and actions match, your child will truly feel treasured.

> **Touch sends a message that requires no words at all.**

One of the most important ways to reach out is through your touch. A child must be touched to feel truly treasured. The power of touch is immeasurable. Many scientific and medical studies show touch is essential to life and that it has healing qualities, but that shouldn't surprise Christians. God has shown its importance and the many ways it can benefit us as he both touches people's hearts and touches them physically. Let's look at some times God touched and why he did so.

Touch Gives Emotional Comfort and Assurance

> Jesus came and touched them [the disciples]. "Get up," he said "Don't be afraid." (Matt. 17:7)

> Look at my hands and feet. It is I myself! Touch me and see. (Luke 24:39)

Then the LORD reached out his hand and touched my mouth. (Jer. 1:9)

BEING OPENLY AFFECTIONATE, VERBALLY AND PHYSICALLY, IS ESSENTIAL.

When we're scared, sad, disappointed, confused, or unsure, one of the most comforting things we can experience is an arm around our shoulder telling us everything will be fine. Our touch can speak confidence, safety, encouragement, and understanding to our children. When we let them know we believe in them and are here to protect and comfort them, they'll feel treasured and secure.

TOUCH BRINGS PHYSICAL HEALING AND STRENGTH

Again the one who looked like a man touched me and gave me strength. (Dan. 10:18)

Jesus reached out his hand and touched the man ... and he was cured. (Mark 1:41–42)

He [Jesus] touched her hand and the fever left her. (Matt. 8:15)

He touched their eyes and ... their sight was restored. (Matt. 9:29–30)

The healing power of touch is still evident today. Many research studies have shown that touch has a physical benefit to people who are sick. Premature babies gain weight faster when they're held, touched, and massaged; blood pressure decreases in people who get appropriate touch; elderly in nursing homes live longer when they're given a pet to touch.[2]

Touch Has Symbolic Meanings

> And he [Jesus] took the children in his arms, put his
> hands on them and blessed them. (Mark 10:16)

Touch sends a message that requires no words at all. The person being touched feels loved, and anyone watching understands this person is special to you. A pat on the back, a quick squeeze, a ruffle of the hair, an arm around his shoulder can all say "You are important to me" and "I love you."

Another action that shows how much you treasure your child is seeking him out. Especially once our children start to move into adolescence, home and family isn't their number one concern. They tend to start spending more of their at-home time in their rooms or on the phone with friends. Taking time to stop by your teen's room just to say hi, to let him know you were thinking about him, can say tons. He may act like he doesn't care, but he will notice and remember.

You can reach out to your child by working to initiate conversation with him. Show him through your actions that you really do care about what he has to say. Take time to stop whatever else you may be doing, get on his level, and look him in the eyes. Learn to ask open-ended questions that will help your child share more than one-word answers.

Encourage your child's dreams.

Studying your child is also important. You should know him well enough to tell when something is bothering him. He may not choose to tell you on his own, but when he realizes you can tell and are interested enough to help draw him out, he'll be more likely to open up because he feels loved.

Being openly affectionate, verbally and physically, is essential to communicate that you treasure your child. Kids need to know they're loved—and they need it most from their parents who are supposed to love them the most. ("If my own parents don't love me, how could anyone else?") It's the foundation of who they are and how they view themselves. If you don't give it to them, they'll look for it elsewhere. Don't slack off on reaching out to your kids!

E—ENCOURAGE

My purpose is that they may be
encouraged in heart and united in love.

—Colossians 2:2

Encouraging your child is showing love through your words. Reaching out to him with your actions, paired with words that match those actions, is an unbeatable combination to prove that you treasure your child. When you encourage him, you build him up emotionally and enhance his self-esteem. You can help him build up his positive qualities by how you talk with him.

Encouragement comes in words of affirmation, appropriate praise, and appreciation. You can encourage your child through simple phrases like: "Thank you," "You're a great kid," "You look great," and "I know you can do it!"

Encouragement reinforces appropriate behavior. When you tell your child "good job" or "I noticed" for activities that often go unnoticed and unappreciated, you strengthen that behavior in your child. Even if we expect certain things from our children, we should never forget to show appreciation when they do them.

Take time every day to tell your child how much you appreciate him. Tell him what you like about him. It bolsters a healthy self-esteem.

It is important *not* to base all your expressions of love on your child's performance. He'll learn to think your love and encouragement is based only on his performance instead of simply who he is.

Encourage your child's dreams, regardless of what you personally think of them. I remember when Taffeta was in about sixth grade, and she and her best friend both wanted to be veterinarians. She came home one day sharing about the plans they'd been making on the playground about starting their own vet clinic together. As Jim listened, he decided this would be a good time to share advice he'd learned from his own life. He proceeded to tell Taffeta that going into business with friends and family wasn't a good idea—disagreements occur and relationships can be damaged. As he shared, you could see Taffeta's dream (and face) begin to deflate. Later, he realized he hadn't chosen a good time to give his business advice. He'd done just the opposite of encouraging her. I noticed him telling her at bedtime that night he didn't mean to discourage her and that he knew if she and Brennen really worked at it, they could have a great vet clinic. Her smile returned.

A—Accept Them Just as They Are

Accept one another, then, just as Christ accepted you,
in order to bring praise to God.

—Romans 15:7

We're each created as individuals; no two are exactly alike. Not only will none of our children be just like their siblings, our kids won't be just like us—thank goodness. To truly treasure our children, we must learn not only to accept these differences, but to embrace them. It's our job to help our kids become their individual selves and develop their own talents. We can't expect a child to grow up accepting himself if we haven't accepted him just as he is.

The foundation of healthy self-esteem is unconditional love, and the basis for unconditional love is true acceptance. Being accepted just as you are, warts and all, and knowing you're loved because of who you are, not what you can do, is the beginning of believing you're important and valued. When you accept your child unconditionally, you commit to loving him no matter what he does, who he marries, or what job he chooses—and relay that commitment to him through your words and actions.

Your child is God's unique and special creation. He has his own set of talents, personality, and interests. Embracing his differences means accepting that different doesn't mean wrong. When you try to mold a child into someone he's not, you send the underlying message he's not good enough just as he is. As you learn to treasure your child and embrace his differences, you'll help him grow his talents to be the very best he can be.

S—SHIELD YOUR CHILD

It [love] always protects.

—1 Corinthians 13:7

When you truly treasure something, you'll do everything in your power to take care of it and protect it from harm. Think of the material possessions you value. Do you park that car you dreamed of for years and now finally own anywhere, vulnerable to the elements of nature and neighborhood animals? Do you leave your family heirloom or favorite collection out for kids to play with and maybe break? Of course not. You'd park at the far end of the parking lot to avoid dings in your doors or cover the heirloom with glass. You do your best to protect your treasure.

You should also do your best to shield and protect your child from things that may harm him. This includes providing basics, such as adequate housing and food, but it also means protecting him from people who may try to hurt him physically or emotionally (bullies, siblings, or unhealthy adults). It includes walking beside him in a dark parking lot and holding him close during a storm. It should also cover shielding him from negative aspects of yourself (mean words, irresponsible behaviors) by working hard to overcome those characteristics we all can show if we aren't careful.

One important facet of shielding your child is knowing when not to. Parents are to protect, but not over-protect. Protecting your child from health hazards, abuse, and other dangers is one thing, but refusing to let him grow up and experience the world, to stretch his wings and try to fly on his own, is completely different. Children who are overly protected from the real world will grow up unprepared and likely resentful. Holding on too tight may only push your child toward rebellion. You need to use wisdom in gauging the right when, where, and how of the letting-go process. But like it or not, you must let go.

Also, protecting your child from the natural and logical consequences of his actions and choices teaches him nothing that will prepare him for reality. The world beyond your home won't be so forgiving. Shielding your child doesn't mean keeping him

> WE SHOULD OBSERVE AND STUDY THE PEOPLE WE LOVE AND LEARN ABOUT WHAT THEY NEED AND WANT FROM US.

from all possible pain. Pain itself can build character, especially when it's directly tied to your child's own choices.

U—UNDERSTAND HIS NEEDS

*Understanding is a fountain of
life to those who have it.*

—*Proverbs 16:22*

We are egocentric creatures who think we know what's best, not only for us, but for everyone else as well. We also seem to believe that everyone else thinks like us, experiences the world as we do, and needs exactly the same things we need. But this is simply not the way it is. We're each individual and unique and will never find anyone truly "just like us." So why do we continually try to give to others and do for others exactly what we'd want them to give to and do for us? If we really understood just how different we are, we'd see how foolish it is to try to meet someone else's needs by doing what we personally need. Instead, we should observe and study the people we love and learn about what they need and want from us. That's what understanding his needs is really all about.

TAKE TIME TO HELP YOUR CHILD SHARE OPENLY WITH YOU WHAT HE NEEDS.

When we're trying to show our children how much we treasure them, we often give them what we think we'd need in that situation—but it's usually the wrong thing. The Golden Rule, "Do to others as you would have them do to you" (Luke 6:31), should be looked at as a general concept, not related to specific behaviors. In general, how do we want others to treat us? We want them to treasure us, treat us with respect, and meet our needs, so that's what we should do for them.

However, if we apply this verse to the specific way to do these things for our family, we'll more often than not miss the mark. For the specific ways we show love and respect to our children to be effective, we'll need to learn what our unique child needs from us and do that. So the Golden Rule for parenting goes more like this:

Do for Your Children as They Need You to Do

If we don't find out specifically what our child needs, we likely won't meet that need. So be sure to take time to help your child share openly with you what he needs from you in different situations. Get into his world and learn how he speaks and receives love. Don't try to read his mind; it will never work. However, you may get close if you read his actions. Observe your child in his interactions at home and with friends and you may get a sense of how he experiences love.

This has definitely proved true in the Cherry household. As Jim and I have observed our three children, we've begun to notice that each of them seems to speak and receive love in completely different ways. Taffeta, our oldest, is all about spending time together. The activity doesn't matter near as much as the fact that we're just together. She'll sit and watch football whether she's interested or not, just to be with us. She requests regular "girl talk" time and loves it when she can go shopping with Mom or to the woods with Dad—especially if it's "just the two of us."

Tiara, on the other hand, focuses on doing things for those

she loves. She's the one who notices that Dad has been out mowing the yard all afternoon and takes him a glass of water. She wants these actions to be her own ideas, unexpected by those around her. She likes the looks of surprise and gratitude she gets from providing these services. She likes to feel important and needed and loves the fact that no one else in the family thought of doing something nice like she did. She's teacher's little helper at school and church and likes being Talon's big sister and helping him do things that he can't do for himself (unless Mom and Dad ask her to help him—then, of course, it's all moans and groans).

IT'S IMPORTANT WE STUDY OUR CHILDREN.

Then Talon, the baby of the family, has been all about absorbing as much physical touch as he possibly can from just about day one. He constantly wants to snuggle, can't seem to sit and watch TV without touching someone, and is known everywhere he goes by the hugs he gives. He not only wants to be in constant contact with everyone around him, he also believes everyone else needs to be touched as much as he does.

This became very obvious one day when he was four. Talon has always had tons of stuffed animals to play with—including a very special bear named Honey Bear that goes everywhere with him just in case he needs a couple of extra hugs when Mom and Dad aren't around. One day, we were cleaning out under his bed (a chore we all just love to do) and found one of his other bears, Cowboy Bear, who had slipped between the bed and the wall. Talon reacted as if he'd been missing for years. He grabbed him and squeezed him with all his might. He carried Cowboy Bear around with him most of the rest of the day. When bedtime arrived, I found Honey Bear had been replaced in Talon's bed, which simply didn't happen. When I asked Talon why he wasn't sleeping with Honey Bear, he said, "Because Cowboy Bear hasn't had enough snuggles yet." Now if that's not a love language, I don't know what is.

Isn't it amazing how three children raised in the same home are so very different in the way they give and receive love? As parents, it's important we study our children and discover exactly how each one experiences love. Otherwise, we may be speaking a language they simply don't understand. In our home, we could spend our time snuggling up with Taffeta, sitting down and talking to Tiara, or doing something nice for Talon—but although those are nice things to do, we wouldn't be adequately meeting each of our individual children's needs.

None of them would actually turn the expression of love away, but it would definitely not mean as much to them as doing something they really received as love.

ℰℭ

OUR CHILDREN ALSO NEED TO FEEL WE RESPECT THEM.

Doing nice things for your child that don't really focus on his personal way of experiencing love is like pouring your love through a colander. As you pour it in, your child will enjoy it briefly, because all of us can experience love in many different ways, but the effects are short-lived as the expression of love quickly drains through the bottom. But once you identify the primary way your child receives love and give that type first and foremost, it's like sealing the holes closed. Then, all the other tokens of love will go in and begin to stay put as an extra dose. When your child's primary language is regularly given first, he begins to fill up and can become filled to overflowing with feeling treasured. When you give and give in ways that don't really speak to your child, he'll likely end up feeling empty. If you take time to really understand your child's needs, your efforts to meet them will be much more successful.

R—Respect Him

Show proper respect to everyone.

—*1 Peter 2:17*

What is *respect?* It's difficult to define, but we all know it when we receive it. But do we know how to give it? As parents, we want and need respect from those around us, including our kids. But our children also need to feel we respect them. We can't "require" our children to respect us, but as we treat them with respect, we're much more likely to receive respect in return.

> Be sure the way you talk to, or about, your children is honoring and considerate.

How do you turn an abstract concept like respect into concrete actions? Let's start with a definition. *Webster's Dictionary* defines respect as: "to hold in high esteem, honor, or reverence; to treat with consideration."[3] Now that's something I think we can work with. If you want your children to feel respected, you'll need to treat them with consideration. You should definitely treat them at least as well as you would anyone else who came to your home.

I think one of the most powerful ways to show a child respect is by teaching him everyone—including him—has good ideas. Take time to ask his opinion about something you're working on or thinking about. Really listen to what he has to say and show him you value his input—then take it a step further. Don't just ask his opinion and then do what you wanted to do anyway; that may make him think you really didn't care what he thought. Instead, if his idea is appropriate, consider actually doing what he suggests. Can you imagine how that might make him feel?

I was discussing this concept with a colleague, and he shared with me how much it would have meant to him. He told me that when he was growing up his dad was the silent type who never interacted with him much. But one day, when he was about thirty years old, his dad asked his opinion about something. "I don't even remember what it was now. All I remember is how that made me feel more valued and important than I'd ever felt before. I remember thinking, 'Why couldn't Dad have ever done that when I was younger?' I always knew he loved me, but that's when I really felt he respected me."

> ESTABLISHING BOUNDARIES IS ALL ABOUT GIVING A CHILD A SENSE OF SECURITY.

You also can show respect to your children by how you communicate with them. Be sure the way you talk to, or about, your children is honoring and considerate. Don't use hurtful or rough language with your kids, and don't tease them about sensitive topics. When you need to correct them, do so with love, mercy, and patience. Don't yell at them, call them names, or label them negatively. Also, consider talking openly with your children about important topics and changes. Keep them in the loop about everything from vacations to moving and anything else you deem appropriate. Letting a child know in advance what's going to happen helps not only his adjustment but also his sense of belonging. Holding family meetings is one great way to keep everyone on the same page.

Need a few more ideas for showing respect to your kids? Try these:

1. Honor their need for privacy.
2. Take one-on-one time with them.
3. Ask them what they want to learn to do, and teach them.
4. Say "I'm sorry" and ask their forgiveness when appropriate.
5. Trust them to make as many of their own decisions as possible.
6. Don't try to change their feelings.

E—ESTABLISH BOUNDARIES

Follow my decrees and be careful to obey my laws,
and you will live safely in the land.

—Leviticus 25:18

Are you surprised to see this as part of making your child feel treasured? Did you think setting up boundaries for your child is really more about discipline and limits than about making a child feel loved and secure? Well, you're partly right. Establishing boundaries does play a significant role in appropriate discipline—but that role is all about giving a child a sense of security.

The Bible says God "disciplines those he loves" (Prov. 3:12). Discipline shows God cares about us enough to keep us from straying off the right path. He has given us clear and unchanging boundaries about right and wrong behavior, clearly defined what we're to do and to avoid doing. Yet, like all children, we test and sometimes blatantly ignore the boundaries. When we go too far and are in harm's way, he pulls us back where we belong.

We also want to keep our children away from danger. To do that, we must establish boundaries around them both physically and figuratively.

When you buy a new home, I'm sure you take time to survey your property boundaries, most likely to clearly understand where your responsibility starts and ends. You know you're responsible for keeping your yard kept up and the area around your home in good condition. Determining where the boundaries are helps you be secure in knowing what's expected of you.

Your child also needs to know the boundaries in his world. Knowing what's required of him and how far he's allowed to go helps create a sense of security in him as well. But to really know for sure he's secure within his boundaries, he must test those limits. He'll go right up and push on them to determine if they're really strong enough to keep him safe. Helping your child know beyond a shadow of a doubt that he's safe and secure, through the boundaries you establish, will definitely help him feel treasured.

Parenting in Practice

It's time to learn how to put the principles of treasuring to work in your life and family. The exercise below works best with children—probably age five and older—who are old enough to write or at least adequately verbalize to you what they want and need. For younger kids, you may be better off just observing their behaviors to determine what makes them feel loved. The older the child, the more you'll glean from this exercise.

"I FEEL LOVED WHEN YOU ..."

In this exercise, you'll have your child create for you the instruction manual for making him feel treasured. Have him write down specific things you can do to make him feel loved. Wouldn't you like to know exactly the right thing to do or say? Remember, good instructional manuals are very specific, with lots of information and detail, so help your child be as clear as possible. The more he writes, the better you'll be able to meet his needs. Describe this to your child as a "wish list." It can include things, activities, and experiences he "wishes" could be part of his world and that would make him feel treasured.

To start, at the top of a piece of paper write, "I feel loved when you ..." Then ask your child to fill the paper with (or tell you verbally) things you could do to make him feel loved. The list should include things from all the following categories:

Things you used to do but don't do anymore. Children hardly ever outgrow some activities, yet we seem to do them less and less. You may find your child still loves to cuddle with you on the couch, have you sing to him at bedtime, or have you read a book to him.

Things you do often. Some tasks we do for our children daily or weekly often become habit or duty. We may have no idea they mean anything special to our children. This became clear to me a few weeks ago when I was talking with Tiara about school. She told me about a little girl she'd seen at recess. She said, "It makes me sad to see her. It's so obvious her parents don't love her at all." I asked her what made her think that, and her reply gave me new energy to keep on keeping on. She said, "Because her hair is never brushed, her clothes are never ironed and they don't even match, and she doesn't smell too good." Well, there you have it. Brushing her hair, ironing her clothes, and reminding her to take a shower became ways Tiara feels loved—and I never even knew it (but I guess I should have, since we know her love language is doing things for others). Finding this out actually changed my attitude about these activities. I'd just seen these as part of my responsibility before, but once I realized it made her feel loved to have matching, ironed clothes and brushed hair, I had a whole new perspective on my "job." Examples of this category would be: "I feel loved when you … make my lunch," "take me to church," or "pray with me."

Things you've never done but your child would like. Remember, this is a wish list. As he makes his list, encourage him to think of things he might like to have you do for him.

As your child writes his list, encourage him to consider time and money. He should be sure to include things on the list that take practically no time at all ("I feel loved when you … give me a hug before I leave for school," "tell me that you love me," "tickle my back," "bring me a Coke."), all the way up to things that take lots of time ("I feel loved when you … fix my favorite dinner," "spend your day off planting flowers with me," "take me on a week-long vacation"). Also encourage him to include things that cost nothing or very little ("I feel loved when you … come to my basketball game," "send me a card in the mail," "bring me a candy bar from the grocery store"), all the way up to things that could cost a fortune. Reminding him at this point that this is a "wish list" and he won't necessarily get everything on the list anytime soon is a good idea ("I feel loved when you … give me my own phone line," "buy me a bright-red Mustang," "take me to Disney World").

Be as specific as possible on this list. Ask your child to give enough details that you'll be sure to get it right. If your son just says, "I feel loved when you make my lunch," he may end up with a PB&J, tuna, or pickle sandwich. Be sure he tells you exactly what he wants. If he says, "I feel loved when you bring me a candy bar from the grocery store," and you come home with an Almond Joy when he really wanted a Butterfinger, you'd see a disappointed face. So don't leave room for guesswork.

Once your child has finished the list, have him give it to you. Go over everything on the list to be sure you completely understand what each item entails. Then, begin doing at least one thing a week off the list for your child. (Often, you may be able to do several things weekly.)

Suggestion: This exercise can be even better when each member of the family does it—even the parents. Depending on your children's ages and their ability to understand this concept, they may like having a similar list from you and from siblings. The more each of us knows how to make each other feel loved, the more treasured we'll all feel.

CHAPTER 4

DO YOU LIKE YOU AS MUCH AS I LIKE YOU?

Building Your Child's Self-Esteem

The baseball game was over and the players were beginning to clear the field so the next game—when our nine-year-old would get her chance to play—could get started. But as Jim and I watched the little athletes finishing up with their coaches, we noticed the parents waiting in the wings for their children to get their snacks. One dad was visibly upset about how the game had gone.

By the look on his face, I was sure he was waiting around to let the coach or ref really have it—but instead, it was his son that received his wrath. Right there in front of God and everybody, this dad berated his son for how he had played. "You just stood out there in the outfield picking grass. What were you thinking? You didn't even see that ball coming until your coach started yelling for you to get it. And I thought we practiced batting this week! You sure couldn't tell by the way you were swinging at anything that came your way." The boy's eyes dropped to the ground and he started shuffling his feet. I felt so sorry for him and wanted to remind his dad it was just a game and the kids are only nine years old, but there was no time. The dad whisked the child to the car, complaining all the way.

A few moments later I noticed another dad greeting his son as he came off the field. The distinction was dramatic. This dad grabbed his son for a quick hug, then took off his ball cap and messed up his hair. All the while, he was telling his little guy how proud he was and what a great game he played. Even when his son pointed out where he'd made a mistake in the game, the dad refused to let that be the focus. With a quick "we can work on that some more this week," he quickly returned the conversation to where the boy had performed well, then offered ice cream to celebrate.

ONE OF YOUR MOST IMPORTANT PARENTAL TASKS IS TO HELP YOUR CHILD GROW UP FEELING LOVED.

I realized that both these boys had been wearing the same-colored shirt; they were on the same team. So it wasn't winning or losing the game that caused the dads' different reactions. I hadn't watched the game and had no idea whether these boys won or lost, but the two fathers had responded very differently to the same outcome. I knew one of these boys was likely to be developing a healthy self-esteem, while the other was on a path to not believing in himself or liking himself very much.

The situation made me sit back and take inventory of how I may have responded to my kids' events. Although I don't ever remember being as critical as dad number one, I knew I never wanted to come across even close. When her game was over, I was sure I'd greet my little athlete with open arms and loving, encouraging words.

One of your most important parental tasks is to help your child grow up feeling loved and secure in who she is. At home, children first learn they're important, valued, and truly cared about. The foundation of who we believe we are and who we'll likely turn out to be comes from our family experiences. Are our needs met? Are we treated with love and respect? Are we encouraged to be the very best we can be, yet accepted when we fall short?

The messages we send our children through our interactions are the basis of that child's developing self-esteem. This process begins as soon as she enters the world and continues throughout the rest of her life, but a child's parents have the first and most impact on how she views herself. When she cries, we respond to meet her needs, and that helps her learn that she's important to us. When she tries to tie her shoes for the first time, we're there to encourage and hug her, letting her know that we believe in her. When she strikes out in baseball, we're there to comfort and assure her she's loved for who she is, not for hitting a home run. And when she makes a really bad choice, we're there to remind her she's loved unconditionally.

SELF-ESTEEM

IS LEARNED.

WHAT IS SELF-ESTEEM?

Self-esteem is how a person views herself. Does she believe she's valuable or see herself as worthless and unlovable? Does she have confidence in her abilities or does she fear failure and, therefore, never try?

Self-esteem is learned. It's the cumulative result of your life's many different experiences. It's the most important building block for emotional health and happiness. If you don't believe me, look at the following results.

Children who grow up with a healthy sense of self-worth seem to be more productive, adventuresome, and self-assured. They're more likely to try new things and are generally more active in extracurricular activities. They perform better academically, are more goal-directed, and enjoy an overall sense of security both in who they are and in the world around them. They relate well to peers, yet are less likely to buckle under peer pressure than their counterparts.

SHOWING YOUR CHILD YOU LIKE YOURSELF SHOWS HER IT'S HEALTHY FOR HER TO LIKE HERSELF.

On the other hand, children who grow up feeling negative about themselves are usually sad, fearful, and irritable. They tend to feel unloved, unproductive, and unworthy. They're more likely to become involved in alcohol, drugs, premarital sex, and delinquency. They show low academic achievement and lack confidence in their abilities.[4]

Parents can do many things to help their kids develop a positive sense of self-worth, but the earlier you start the easier it is. It's much easier to build positive self-esteem than to repair a damaged sense of self. Wherever you are in the parenting process, the time to start helping your child to build a strong and healthy sense of self is today!

WAYS TO DEVELOP HEALTHY SELF-ESTEEM IN YOUR CHILDREN

MODEL HEALTHY SELF-ESTEEM

Feel good about your own strengths and accomplishments. Showing your child you like yourself shows her it's healthy for her to like herself. When she hears you talk positively about yourself and your accomplishments and experience joy from them, she'll learn feeling good about yourself is appropriate. If you don't like yourself and talk down about your abilities, your child will learn to do the same. As discussed in the last chapter, you can't give what you don't possess. Trying to teach your child to accept a compliment when she hears you negating compliments that come your way is very difficult. The more you live what you want your child to learn, the better she'll learn it.

GIVE APPROPRIATE AND REALISTIC PRAISE

As you learn to praise your child, I want you to understand there are a couple of "don'ts."

First, *don't be unrealistic.* Your children have a sense about the reality of things, and if your praise doesn't measure up they'll struggle to trust what you say. Telling your B student she's a genius or the smartest kid in class will eventually have a negative outcome. Either she'll truly believe she's the smartest kid in the class and experience social

> **REALISTIC PRAISE SHOULD SIGNIFICANTLY OUTNUMBER NEGATIVE COMMENTS.**

and academic problems when she doesn't perform as a genius, or she may realize she really isn't, but feel pressure to live up to what you believe about her. Either way, her self-esteem ends up more negative than before—which was never the intention of the praise in the beginning. So keep your praise accurate and true and focused on her positive and unique traits, talents, and abilities.

Second, *don't overindulge your child in praise.* If children are constantly showered with praise for every little thing they do, you may end up with a praise addict—someone who associates her sense of self-worth with how much praise she can acquire.

COMPARING ONE CHILD'S DIFFICULTIES WITH ANOTHER CHILD'S STRENGTHS DAMAGES THE CHILD'S SELF-ESTEEM.

She'll likely become an approval-seeker who'll do whatever necessary to receive praise by those around her. She won't develop a strong sense of identity because she'll be too busy pleasing others. She'll have difficulty standing up to peer pressure, regardless of her personal values and morals, because that may result in rejection she's not equipped to handle. This approval-seeking may lead her either to overachieving to gain her parents' or peers' approval, or to underachieving, realizing she could never meet their expectations and giving up.

Finally, *don't invalidate her feelings.* Allow your child to express her own hurts and disappointments about a particular event or situation. When Julie has had a bad day on the soccer field, failed a test at school, or told a lie and she's feeling disappointed in herself, listen to her. This isn't the time to respond with, "I thought you played great today," "Well, maybe math just isn't your subject, but you're great at science," or any other invalidating praise statement. She knows herself, and if she's feeling disappointed she needs you to validate that feeling, then help her figure out how to perform better next time.

The biggest don't of praising is *don't forget to praise your child!* Overall, she needs to hear what you like about her, how special she is, and what you think she's doing well. So often, parents are quick to tell a child what she's done wrong but don't stop to tell her something she did right or let her know they're glad she's their daughter for no particular reason at all.

Our realistic praise should significantly outnumber negative comments and corrections we make at least five or ten to one.

Keep Expectations Realistic

Whether or not we openly tell a child what we expect from her, she'll know. Our nonverbal as well as verbal responses inform a child what types of behaviors we approve of and which ones we don't. Children will feel pressure to live up to what's expected of them, so be sure those expectations are realistic.

Many parents don't take time to consider what they expect from their child until the expectation isn't met. Then they may loudly express what they'd wanted with feelings of disappointment and anger. So first, consider your expectations and whether they're realistic for your child. Do her skills, developmental stage, intellectual development, and environment allow your expectations to be met? If not, adjust them to an appropriate level for your child.

Once you've determined realistic expectations, tell your child what you anticipate from her. You can help her feel good about herself by giving her opportunities for success. It breeds success to know exactly what's expected of you and that you're capable of doing it; then all you have to do is do it. Success feels good, so set your child up for it by assigning her age-appropriate chores and responsibilities. She'll also be contributing to the family and feeling useful and productive.

Identify and Applaud Your Child's Unique Qualities

Each child is a unique and beautiful creation with a distinctive personality, temperament, talents, and skills. No two are alike, and we shouldn't try to make them be. Each child also has her own idiosyncratic areas of difficulty. No child is perfect. Comparing one child's difficulties with another child's strengths, inside or outside the family, damages the child's self-esteem.

Instead, get to know your child's unique strengths and qualities and applaud them. A child may view something "different" about herself as "wrong" or "bad," and other children will do their best to help that thinking along by picking up on the "different" trait and teasing her about it. It's the parents' job to counter this thinking by helping our child see how "different" can be wonderful and cool. We can help her appreciate her differences and see these as strengths or blessings, and we can let her know we love her uniqueness.

Sometimes your child may wish she weren't quite so "unique," especially around her peers (no matter how celebrated that difference may be at home), and she may be struggling to fit in and feel normal. When this happens, be sensitive to your child's feelings and help her through this compassionately. Such encounters seem most evident in those preadolescent and adolescent years when everything seems to be changing. Children develop at different rates, so parents need to be sensitive to how difficult this time is for our children and do what we can to help and not hurt their self-esteem.

I just about messed up big in such a situation with Taffeta. She was eleven years old, and we were headed to the mall to shop for school clothes for the start of her sixth-grade adventure. She was excited about our yearly shopping trip and became even more so when she realized she and Mom were going alone, with no brother or sister tagging along. This time was just for her, and she had some very specific plans for her new wardrobe—although she hadn't yet shared them with me.

As we hit the first store, I noticed some unexpected apprehension in Taffeta, but when I asked her about it she shrugged it off, saying she was just thinking about what she needed and wanted to buy. Since she's always been a bit of a worrier and list-maker, this sounded reasonable to me. I could just imagine her rummaging through her closet and drawers in her mind to take inventory of what still fit and how many new shirts and jeans she thought she needed—but I soon found out her list included more than shirts and jeans.

We had picked out, tried on, put back, and purchased several items in the first couple of stores and were in the third when I noticed that apprehension again. Taffeta had finished trying on several things, and as I was going to put the ones she didn't want back on the rack, she informed me she'd meet me around the corner and took off ahead of me. I finished what I was doing and headed to where she said she'd be.

As I rounded the corner, I saw my little baby standing in front of a bra display—and my world began to shake. You need to understand that Taffeta was a *very* small (in every sense of the word) eleven-year-old girl. She was short, skinny, and tiny. While many of her friends were moving out of the children's department into the stores' juniors sections, Taffeta was still wearing a little-girls' size seven. She'd often complained about her stature, only to hear from me and other adult women, "Enjoy it while you can. Millions of women would give anything to be petite and skinny." (Yes, now I realize that was a very insensitive and invalidating statement.) I knew she didn't like the fact she wasn't growing like her peers, but that didn't occur to me at the time. All I could think was that my little girl was trying to grow up too quickly and I had to put a stop to it! (After all, I wasn't sure I wanted her to grow up at all.)

For the next few minutes, I was an insensitive and unobservant parent. "What do you think you're doing over here?" (As if I didn't know.)

"Do you think I could get a bra before school starts?"

"I don't think that's really necessary, do you? You don't even need a bra yet. I promise you it's nothing great to have to wear one. I wish you'd stop trying to grow up so fast."

The look in Taffeta's eyes pierced right through my heart. And as her chin dropped to her chest, I knew immediately I'd made a terrible blunder. Without even trying, I'd just embarrassed, humiliated, and invalidated my daughter in less than thirty seconds. As quickly as I could, I reached out to Taffeta to hug her and apologize, but it was too late. She pulled away with tears in her eyes and said, "Never mind, I was just wondering." Boy, was I going to have some major making-up to do.

The joy of our shopping day together was quickly going down the drain, and if I was going to salvage it at all, I'd better think fast. I took Taffeta's face in my hands and more sincerely than before explained how sorry I was for being a totally insensitive grown-up. I told her I understood that when we don't have something everyone else seems to have, we seem to want it all the more—and since I was in the already-have group, I'd forgotten what it was like to be in the still-waiting-to-have group. Taffeta was beginning to smile both at the humor of my descriptions and at watching her mom sweat her way out of this situation. This time, my request for forgiveness was granted and met with a hug and a "Now can I have that bra?" I bought her two.

> **WOULD YOU FEEL YOU'RE SPECIAL TO SOMEONE WHO NEVER INTERACTED WITH YOU?**

CELEBRATE YOUR CHILD

Taking time out of your busy schedule to remember and celebrate special occasions, recognize milestones, and acknowledge things she has done are a few of the many ways to make your child feel special. Celebrate birthdays. After all, that's the day your life was blessed by this very special bundle you now can't imagine living without. Make sure she knows it by celebrating the day God gave you one of the best gifts ever.

GET ON YOUR CHILD'S LEVEL AND PLAY, DO, OR TALK ABOUT WHATEVER'S INTERESTING TO HER.

In the Cherry home, we celebrate natural birthdays and also commemorate each child's "Christian birthday." All three of our kids became Christians at very early ages, and we've worked to help them remember by celebrating and talking about the day that happened. This has become a very special time for the whole family, and the kids are learning not only about their own, but also their siblings' special day.

Here are a few more ways to celebrate your children:

1. Create a personalized scrapbook of memories.
2. Tell your child stories about her life that are unique to her—the day she came into your family, what happened, how you felt the first time you held her, etc. Kids love to hear these.
3. Make up a special song or story that's just hers.
4. Give fun nicknames.
5. Create family traditions: baking cookies, carving jack-o'-lanterns, shooting off fireworks, etc.

INTERACT WITH YOUR CHILD EVERY DAY

If you want your child to grow up with healthy self-esteem, you'll need to be involved in her life. Would you feel you're special to someone who never interacted with you? Your child must receive daily attention from you to feel good about herself.

You may interact in different ways depending on your child's age, development, and needs. The most important thing is to get on your child's level and play, do, or talk about whatever's interesting to her. This isn't the time for teaching, instructing, correcting, or directing. Let your child lead, and show her what she wants to do or talk about is very important to you, too.[5]

PARENTING IN PRACTICE

Do you wonder how your child feels about herself? Can you tell how healthy her self-esteem is? You may have an idea simply from observation, but if you want more, here's a short quiz to help you find out. Give it to your child (or read it to her) to find out what she's thinking.

This is not a professional, standardized test; it's simply a quiz that may give you and your child insight as to how she's doing and where you can help her continue to grow. There are no right or wrong answers; she's simply stating whether or not a particular statement describes her more often than not. Use it as a guideline and a way to initiate conversation with your child about something few of us ever discuss.

HOW I FEEL ABOUT ME

Take a minute to consider each statement below and answer true or false (honestly) as to whether or not that statement describes you most of the time.

1. I like who I am . . . . T   F
2. I like to try new things . . . . T   F
3. I am proud of my accomplishments . . . . T   F
4. I can accept a compliment with a
   "thank you" . . . . T   F
5. I feel loved and accepted by my family . . . . . T   F

6. I'm able to forgive myself when I mess up. . . T F
7. I usually learn from my mistakes and
   try to do things differently next time . . . . T F
8. I can accept others giving me suggestions
   about how to do things differently . . . . T F
9. I generally believe I'm just as good as my
   peers (not better than or worse than them). . T F
10. I usually believe I can achieve whatever
    I set my mind to do. T F
11. I have goals for my future and believe
    I'm capable of reaching them . . . . T F
12. I rarely worry about how things will
    work out . . . . T F
13. I choose not to dwell on my setbacks
    or failures for long. T F
14. I feel comfortable stating my own
    thoughts and opinions to my peers . . . . T F
15. I know who I am and what I believe
    and can stand up for those things. . . . . T F
16. I'm not like anyone else, and I am
    comfortable with that . . . . T F
17. I rarely feel sad or fearful for no reason . . . . . T F
18. I believe I'm important and valuable
    to my parents . . . . T F
19. I rarely feel like I'd like to be somebody else. . . T F
20. I know how to figure out solutions
    to problems . . . . T F
21. I can do things for myself . . . . T F
22. I know the things I'm not so good at,
    and I'm OK with those things. . . . . T F
23. I can take credit for good things I had
    something to do with . . . . T F
24. I don't take blame for things that
    aren't my responsibility. . . . . T F

CHAPTER 5

A CHILD SPELLS LOVE T-I-M-E

Understanding the Power of Quality and Quantity Time

We live in a very busy world, and most of us are running one hundred miles per hour to keep up. There still are only twenty-four hours in a day, but we're cramming more than ever into those precious hours. Something will suffer if we're not careful, and odds are it will be our families. Let's look at the issue of quality vs. quantity time—and since we have so little time, we'd better get started.

QUALITY OR QUANTITY?

This has been an issue for years. Do our kids really need so much of our time? Or do they really just need "quality" time with us? We don't seem to ponder the quantity vs. quality question in any other areas of our lives, so why is it such a big issue in our families?

One night Jim and I were celebrating our anniversary, and he wanted to take me out to a really nice restaurant. He'd picked one of the most expensive places in town, and I was thrilled—until I saw the menu and the prices. I wanted to politely excuse ourselves, but Jim assured me it was fine and we were going to order the best in the house—after all, his bride was worth it.

We worked our way through the menu of things we'd never heard of (I'm really a hamburgers-and-hot-dogs kind of girl), asked our waiter ridiculous (and apparently irritating) questions, and finally settled on the waiter's favorite of some sort of fish in some kind of seaweed wrap or something like that. It was going to cost a fortune, but we were treating ourselves and knew we'd be getting the best-quality whatever-it-was that Springfield had to offer. Our expectations were high—and then dinner arrived. In front of each of us sat a plate of four tiny pinwheels and a couple of cutesy garnishes to help make the plate look full.

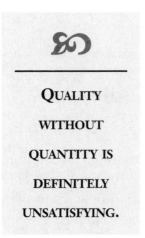

QUALITY WITHOUT QUANTITY IS DEFINITELY UNSATISFYING.

Jim was sure it must be our appetizer (even though, at those prices, we chose not to order an appetizer) and called our waiter over. No, it really was our dinner of the finest-quality fish available. I'm sure it would have been wonderful if there were enough to even taste it. "Oh, well," I smiled, "it's the quality not the quantity that really matters, right?" Jim didn't see the humor and was frustrated at paying that price for practically nothing. In his mind, when we decide to spend our hard-earned cash going out to eat, he wants to get the most for his money. One or two bites of the highest-quality anything just doesn't cut it.

Do you think our kids often feel like that? Frustrated at waiting forever for just a little taste of time with their parents? Then they have to try to be satisfied with the "quality" of time and not disappointed in the quantity. Overall, quality without quantity is definitely unsatisfying. What everyone, especially children, really wants is a large quantity of high-quality time.

They really do need both! They need quality time with their parents—and lots of it!

I'm afraid the whole quality vs. quantity issue is really just a way for parents to relieve their guilt for not truly giving their children either. We get so busy with jobs and outside activities that we leave little to no time for our kids. Then we try to soothe ourselves by rationalizing that just a little quality time here and there will be good enough. We plan a big, two-week vacation once a year. Then we spend those two weeks running ourselves and our kids crazy trying to force all the fun we possibly can into a short amount of time. We're trying to make up for lost time and store up extra time for the following year. This just doesn't work.

Yes, vacations are great, but they can't be the only time you choose to make your family a priority. Your kids need you year round in regularly scheduled doses. We need to focus on improving the quantity of our quality time together.

Research shows kids need both quality and quantity time with parents and that kids with parents who are actively involved in their lives are less likely to have social, emotional, or academic problems; use drugs or alcohol; be involved in crime; or engage in premarital sex.[6] But unfortunately, it seems kids aren't getting what they need. Time is in short supply in our society. Consider these recent research findings:

- Family dinners have decreased 33%
- Family vacations are down 28%
- Study time has increased 50%
- Household conversations dropped drastically between 1981 and 1997
- Structured sports more than doubled; passive/spectator sports increased five times
- Nearly 50% of school-aged children don't come home to a parent

- U.S. parents spend less time with their children than almost any other nationality
- The average American home has the TV on 49 hours per week, but meaningful parent-child conversations fill only 39 minutes per week
- Religious participation is down 40% for ages three to twelve and 24% for high-school students[7]

These are sad statistics, especially when you consider that past research indicated having family meals together was the strongest predictor of academic success, avoidance of undesirable behavior, and better nutrition.[8] We seem to be doing everything we can to set up our children for failure. We may not *plan* to neglect our families, but if we don't *plan* time together, it won't happen. Families don't *find* time to be together, they *make* time to be together. As the parent, you're responsible for making this time together a priority.

> OUR KIDS DON'T NEED ALL THESE EXTRA ACTIVITIES AS MUCH AS THEY NEED FAMILY TIME.

It's time to evaluate just how much time your family actually spends together. Where exactly is all your time and energy going? How do you spend your free time? Are your kids so busy after school they don't have time for dinner at home? Do you seem to be going different directions every evening? How many free evenings do you have in a week?

Our society is pushing us to get our kids involved in every possible extracurricular activity. If you don't, you're viewed as a bad parent for not giving your children these opportunities. In reality, our kids don't need all these extra activities as much as they need family time and down time to do nothing. For the first time in history, we're raising kids who experience burnout before they graduate from high school. We must learn to set priorities in order and budget our time accordingly—and we must learn to slow down.

THE PRIORITY LADDER

Priorities are much like rungs on a very tall ladder. Everything in our lives occupies a rung, the top rungs being the most important or pressing at the moment, and the lower rungs less pressing. For example, right now the number one rung for me is writing this section about priorities (number one for you would be reading it). But my ladder doesn't have only one rung on it. Taking my kids to their gymnastics class might be about rung six, watching a good football game about eighteen, and changing closets from summer clothes to winter clothes around one hundred seventy-three. Everything fits somewhere, and eventually, most things get a chance to occupy the number one spot. (When I get around to changing those closets sometime next century, it will be first for a moment or two.)

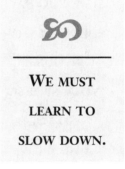

WE MUST LEARN TO SLOW DOWN.

Some things in our lives tend to occupy that coveted number one spot fairly regularly, and these things need to be identified and evaluated. The top five things on your priority ladder alternate easily into the first position and are therefore the most valued and important to you. One way to evaluate what your top five are is to look through your checkbook and your calendar. Where we spend our time and our money will tell us what we value.

Things you may find in your top five might include: job, school, children, religion, recreation, spouse, self, cleaning, friends, and hobbies. As you identify your priorities, it's important to remember the top five are all fairly equal in their importance to you. At any given moment, depending on circumstances, any of these five could take precedence. You

YOU SHOULD BE SURE YOU HAVE ADEQUATE TIME FOR YOURSELF, YOUR SPOUSE, AND YOUR CHILDREN.

may be working out at the gym when the school calls to tell you little Brian has fallen off the monkey bars and is hurt. Very quickly your top priority moves from self time to taking care of your child. Or you may be on a date with your spouse and get an emergency call from work. Again, the number one spot changes from spouse to work. The problem arises when you evaluate your priorities honestly and find that people and things that *should* be most important don't make the top-five list.

EVALUATING YOUR PRIORITIES

Take a few minutes right now to grab a piece of paper and write down what you believe to be your top five priorities. This isn't the time to write down the "right" answer (we all know what "should" be there). Be honest with yourself. Where do you spend most of your time, energy, and money? What do your *behaviors* say is most valuable to you? Think about it this way. If I followed you around for one or two weeks recording how you spent your time, what conclusions might I draw about your priorities?

Now that you've honestly identified your top five priorities, it's time to evaluate them. Is there anything there that surprises you? More important, is anything *not* there that should be? As parents, you should be sure you have adequate time for yourself, your spouse, and your children. Are all three of these in your top five? If any one of them isn't there, you or someone in your home likely isn't satisfied with how things are measuring up.

One of the biggest priority-setting mistakes I see is parents not putting themselves in the top five—either individually for self time or as a team for couple time. When this happens, it may indicate your children and their activities are eating up more than their fair share of the top spots. I promise you you'll be better parents if you take care of yourself and your marriage along the way. Focusing totally on the children is dangerous for everyone involved (see my book, *Childproofing Your Marriage*). To have a happy and healthy home, you need to take time away from the children to do your own thing and spend adult time together, just the two of you.

Another priority problem I see seems to be just as prevalent as the first in many homes today: Parents make sure they're in the top five priorities, but their children are not. Now, these parents desperately want to believe their kids are the most

Start making time for each other right now.

important thing to them. After all, "That's why I work such long hours ... so I can give those kids everything I never had." I'm here to tell you those kids would much rather have parents than new toys. Putting yourself as one of the top five rungs on the ladder and *not* putting your children in there means trouble. You're being selfish, focused more on what *you* want than on what your family needs.

Go back now and look at your top-five list. Let's assume that your relationship with God is in the number one slot (if it's not, you should strongly consider making it number one!). After that, check to see if these three important priorities (self, spouse, and children) are there. If one or more is not, continue down the rungs of your priority ladder writing things in until you see all three on the list. How far did you have to go? What does this tell you about changes that need to be made?

BUDGETING OR SETTING PRIORITIES HELPS YOU MAKE SURE THAT YOU GET THE BIGGEST AND MOST IMPORTANT THINGS DONE FIRST.

MAKING TIME

Ways to make time for your child include: adjusting your schedule to be at his activities, teaching him to mow the yard (even when you could do it quicker alone), calling him on the phone when you're away, and tucking him in bed. Even recognizing our time is limited, we can make the most of the time we do have with our children. Happy, healthy families don't find time to be together, they make time to be together. I challenge you to start making time for each other right now. Make it your number one priority to ensure your family (spouse and children) knows and feels they're number one to you.

These suggestions for creating quality family time together can help get you started.

1. Plan "dates" with each of your children.
2. Work on a family scrapbook together.
3. Start family traditions.
4. Celebrate special occasions and milestones.

5. Turn chores into games and do them together.
6. Eat together with the TV off. Talk about your day.
7. Let your child be in charge of the activities for an evening.
8. Play games together instead of watching TV.

BUDGETING TIME

You just completed the first step to making better use of your time—deciding what's really most important to you. If you didn't like your honest evaluation of your current priorities, it's time to decide what you really want in those top five spots. This will help you as you begin step two: budgeting your time.

Setting priorities is much like financial budgeting. You understand you have a limited supply of money and it's going to go somewhere. Taking time to budget your money means you're actively choosing where your money will be spent. If you don't do this, you'll likely spend bits of money here and there; then when it's time to pay the big bills, you don't have enough left over.

BE WILLING TO SAY NO TO GOOD THINGS TO LEAVE TIME FOR THE BEST THING.

The same principle applies to time. You have only twenty-four hours in a day, and that time will be spent doing something. You can actively choose where you spend your time or not; it's up to you. But if you don't budget your time, you may find your day, week, or month eaten away by trivial and less-important things. Then, when you need to spend time with someone or something that's really important to you, there may not be any time left over. Budgeting or setting priorities helps you make sure that you get the biggest and most important things done first. When we're careful to fit the biggest and most important things into our lives first, we find there's room for more. However, if we first fill our lives with all the little things, there's no way to fit in all the big things in life.

LEARNING TO SLOW DOWN

How do you slow down and commit to a less-hectic lifestyle that will allow you and your children more time together? Here are a few suggestions:

1. Avoid overscheduling by setting limits to how many activities both you and your children are involved in at any one time. Be as willing to give up some of your hobbies or activities as you want your children to be.

2. Preserve family time; make it intentional. Put it on the calendar—in ink! As your children see you making family time important to you, they'll see it as important as well.

3. Set new and realistic expectations. The house doesn't have to be spotless; meals don't have to be gourmet.

4. Set a routine for daily activities and chores. Making a schedule helps keep everyone on task. Household chores will get done more regularly. When we avoid letting things pile up, we realize these activities can actually take less time than we thought. That frees up additional time to spend with each other.

5. Turn off the TV. The number of quality family shows available is minimal, anyway. So why waste time when you could be enjoying each other's company?

6. Be willing to say no to good things to leave time for the best thing: quality family time.

7. Set aside fifteen minutes a day to let your child be

the boss. Let him be in charge of the topic or activity without your controlling it, making suggestions, or teaching. If you have several children, consider letting each of them be king (or queen) for one evening. Let them choose what's for dinner, who does what chores, and the after-dinner activity.

8. Involve kids in chores. If you have to run errands, take one of the kids with you and enjoy some one-on-one time together.

9. Consider becoming a one-income family or switching to a part-time job. Although this initially may seem to some an unreasonable option, it is actually more doable than one might think. Yes, it does take some sacrifice and a willingness to value time more than things, but it also frees up budget money that would otherwise be spent on upkeep for that second career. Perhaps that second car would no longer be necessary, nor would quarterly purchases of new work clothes, nor frequent fast-food dinner expenses, and so on. It's certainly an option worth considering.

10. Use time-savers and short-cuts whenever possible.[9]

Spending time together is a powerful way to show your child love. We can't measure love, but we can and do measure time. If time equals love, how are you measuring up? Do you seek out opportunities to spend time with your child? Or are you so busy going to work, cleaning the house, doing the laundry, mowing the yard, and shopping for food that you miss chances for spontaneous interactions that say, "I love you?" How often do you find yourself saying, "In a minute"? Does a minute drag into hours and days?

If we aren't careful, activities we believe we "must" and "should" do eat up all our time, and our children are the ones who pay. I learned this lesson early and have tried to prevent the problem ever since.

THE DAY A MINUTE LASTED F-O-R-E-V-E-R

Taffeta was a little more than three years old and always looked forward to our "stay-home" days. This is what she called weekends, because she didn't have to go to the sitter's house and got to stay home with her family. In the past, these stay-home days were usually full of attention for her from both her parents. We'd take turns playing or reading with her, while the other got a few chores done. This was working fine until her little sister came along and started stealing much of the time on which Taffeta had once held a monopoly. Shortly after that, Taffeta decided she needed to learn to tell time.

Early one Saturday morning, Taffeta had tired of *VeggieTales* and decided it was time to read a book. She picked one of her favorites and headed to find me. Unfortunately, I was busy feeding the time-thief named Tiara, and Taffeta heard the first of what would eventually be many references to something called a minute. "In just a minute, sweetie. I'm feeding Tiara."

> **I REALIZED THAT FROM HER PERSPECTIVE A "MINUTE" WAS A WHOLE DAY LONG.**

Taffeta took it in stride and ran off to find her favorite doll. She got distracted and forgot all about the book, at least for a while. Later that morning, she came to me again, book in hand, and a big smile on her face. She was sure that thing called a minute must be over by now. But when she asked again that time—and several more times throughout the day—she found out she was wrong.

"Just a minute; I've got to finish these dishes."

"I've got to lay Tiara down for a nap. We'll do that in just a minute."

"I'm on the phone. I'll read you a book in just a minute."
As evening approached, she tried one more time. Jim and
I were sitting at the table talking (about something very
important, I'm sure). Taffeta walked in, book in hand, but the
smile was long gone by now. When she asked to read the
book, she was again met with the now infamous minute. "Yes,
sweetheart, we'll read that in just a minute; Mommy and
Daddy are talking." She turned on her heel with her hand on
her hip and said, "A minute is F-O-R-E-V-E-R!"

That stopped me dead in my tracks, and the day flashed
quickly before my eyes. As I saw her look of disappointment,
I realized how many times I had put her off for "more important" things. And I realized that from her perspective a
"minute" was a whole day long. Needless to say, I felt horri-
ble and immediately began working to restore my
relationship with this little hurt soul. I decided that day that I
never wanted to put off my children like that again.

Of course, I haven't kept that decision perfectly, but since
that day I've been much more aware when I do try to get one
of the kids to wait "just a minute." I know I can't just drop
everything to do whatever the kids want whenever they
want, but I can do much better at responding to their desires
in a reasonable time. I now work very hard so my kids don't
have to hear "just a minute" more than twice (or preferably
once). If I find myself starting to say it for the third time, I
quickly take inventory of what I'm choosing over spending
time with my child. Short of an emergency, I stop what I'm
doing and join my child in the activity he or she is choosing.

Parenting in Practice

Budgeting Your Time

The first step in time budgeting is to find out where your time is going. To do this, keep a time journal for one week, especially of nonwork hours, of how you and your family spend your time. See who is doing what and going where.

The next step is a family meeting. Find time to sit down as a family (if the children are old enough to participate) at the end of the week and discuss your findings. Talk about where each member feels family time should be spent and their personal priorities in this area. Then have each member rank the activities from most to least important to them, and discuss ways to fit in the most important things and do away with some of the least important activities.

Try these adjustments for about thirty days, then regroup and discuss how the changes are working. If adjustments are still needed or if some priorities have changed, talk through these issues and decide what needs to be done. You may find your family needs to meet regularly to keep up with changing schedules and activities. That's not a bad idea. The point is that we communicate a desire to spend time together and do whatever is necessary to make that happen.

CHAPTER 6

MONKEY SEE, MONKEY DO

The Power of Modeling

An evangelist at a revival my family was attending was challenging the adults to be better parents, explaining that children are much more likely to do as they see their parents doing than what parents tell them to do. He drove this point home with a story that has stuck with me to this day. He spoke of a young man we'll call "Shawn," a fairly talented basketball player. He was in his senior year of high school and generally popular around their small community. The evangelist knew him from church, which Shawn and his family attended fairly regularly. The preacher listed several more positive traits about Shawn—it seemed he was the "all-American kid."

Then the story became sad. The evangelist received a phone call late one night from Shawn's father stating that Shawn had been killed in a tragic, one-car accident. He immediately went to be with the family, and they cried and prayed together. A couple of days before the funeral, the family was told significant amounts of alcohol were found in Shawn's blood. Everyone was shocked. "Not Shawn! How could this happen?" The answer came just a few weeks later.

The evangelist got a call one evening from Shawn's mother, asking him to come over right away. When he arrived at the home he found the dad collapsed on the kitchen floor, crying uncontrollably. As he tried to console him, he noticed a small piece of paper clenched tightly in the distraught father's hand. As he pried it loose and read it, he realized what was tormenting this father. The note was in Shawn's handwriting and had been found in the back of one of the kitchen cabinets, where the parents kept a few bottles of alcohol. The note simply said, "Dad, IOU one bottle of booze. Shawn."

> AS CHRISTIAN PARENTS, WE OFTEN MUST EVALUATE OURSELVES AND WHAT OUR LIVES ARE MODELING.

That tragic story isn't the only one of its kind. Children all over the world are following in their parents' footsteps down some very destructive roads. Whether it's alcohol and drugs, unhealthy relationships, abuse, dishonesty, irresponsibility, disrespect for authority, or any of a million other life issues, children learn it first from their parents. It doesn't really matter much what you tell your children about these issues; what matters is what you show them through your own behavior. What are your children seeing?

We all learned much of what we know and do by example. We learn how to do things by watching people who already know how to do them. As Christ is the example for Christians to follow, parents are children's example. "Do as I say, not as I do" should be stricken from our thoughts and minds. We all know that what we as parents *do* is far more likely to be imitated than what we *say*. As Christian parents, we often must evaluate ourselves and what our lives are modeling to those who are watching us closely—our children.

ACTIONS SPEAK LOUDER THAN WORDS

One morning, a mother was running late getting herself and her daughter out of the house. She had been rushing, pushing, and prodding all morning, and they were finally on the road, but quite late. Her daughter was aware of her mother's frustration and, while they were driving to her preschool, suggested her mother drive faster. Mom, seeing an opportunity to teach respect for the law, responded she simply could not go faster than the speed limit. The preschooler sat quietly for a minute, then said, "Maybe you should get a car like Daddy's. It has a faster speed limit."

Whether or not we realize it, children are always watching. They notice the littlest things, and as a result begin to form opinions of what's right and wrong. We may be actively trying to teach with our words, but we must also teach with our actions. Parents must learn to say what they mean and live what they say. There's no room for double standards in parenting. Children will learn lessons we teach with our actions much better and remember them much longer. We are our most powerful teaching tool.

> **PARENTS MUST LEARN TO SAY WHAT THEY MEAN AND LIVE WHAT THEY SAY.**

Our children become avid parent-watchers at birth and learn things long before they can speak or understand language. If you think you'll have to wait until you can talk to your children to start teaching what they should and shouldn't do, you'll be way behind; your children started learning long before you realized you were teaching through every move you make.

Parents lead by example and expect young children to "do what I do." Much of this teaching seems to come naturally; we don't even realize we're doing it. Have you ever tried to feed a baby without opening your own mouth as the spoon is headed for hers? When our kids are young, we're thrilled when they do what we do. We teach them to wave bye-bye, blow kisses, make funny faces, or show how old they are simply by doing those actions over and over in front of them. As they get older, we model things like how to dress and feed ourselves, how to hold a baby doll, and how to throw a ball.

OUR CHILDREN WATCH HOW WE MANAGE LIFE'S OBSTACLES, CHALLENGES, AND DAILY EVENTS.

These outward behaviors are taught both intentionally and unintentionally, but as our kids get older, we teach fewer outward behaviors and more inward/character traits. These are harder to notice right away, but they're definitely being taught and learned. We teach things like honesty, responsibility, respect, and values whether or not we ever sit our children down and talk to them about these topics. About this stage, our children's mimicking of our behaviors somehow ceases to be cute. Why do we work so hard to get our children to do what we do—then later get them into trouble for it? That must be quite confusing to them.

DO YOU WALK THE TALK?

- Do you tell your kids to tell a caller you're not home when you are—then tell your children not to lie?
- Do you buy a child's-price ticket when your child is older—then tell your child to always be honest?
- Do you drive faster than is legal with your child in the car with you—then tell your child to obey the law?

- Do you treat your spouse disrespectfully—then tell your child, "Don't talk to your mom (or dad) that way"?
- Do you talk negatively about your boss or pastor behind his back—then tell your child to show respect for authority?
- Do you do most of the work on a project that has your child's name on it—then tell your child not to cheat?
- Do you borrow things from work and "forget" to return them—then tell your child stealing is wrong?

These are just a few examples of where our actions say more than we know. Our children watch how we manage life's obstacles, challenges, and daily events. They learn from every decision they watch us make, and their respect for us will either grow or disappear depending on how close our actions match our words. They won't respect and, therefore, won't want to imitate a hypocrite.

Children are given role models everywhere: in peers, teachers, and movie stars; from television, sports, music, and books. If we don't live what we believe, it won't be hard for our kids to find someone who does—but we may not approve of what they believe. If you want to teach your child that what you believe is vital, make sure your actions show just how vital those things really are to you.

What Is Your Marriage Teaching?

As your child grows and learns about the world, she learns from each parent individually. But as she begins to learn about relationships between people, especially male-female relationships, she'll study your marriage and how the two of you interact. She's watching even when you think she isn't. She notices private exchanges and looks. She learns about how couples make decisions together and resolve conflict. She learns how she can be expected to be treated someday by members of the opposite sex. She learns what marriage really means and how it works—from how to argue, how to show affection, and how to work as a team, to how to divide chores and household responsibilities.

What my children are learning about the roles of men and women in the home became very evident to me one day. We were all home for the evening and I was putting in a load of clothes to wash—something I rarely do because that's a job Jim has taken on in our household. While I was in the laundry room, I heard a little voice calling, "Mommy, where are you?" I answered Talon and told him where I was. As he rounded the corner, I saw his confused look and asked what was wrong. He said, "I was looking for you. I looked everywhere you're supposed to be and couldn't find you. Why are you back here? That's Daddy's job." I had to laugh as I explained Mommy and Daddy can both do most of the jobs around the house, but he was right it was "Daddy's job."

Without our ever stating anything about the division of labor in the house, Talon had decided which jobs were Daddy's jobs and which Mommy's. He had learned something we had never intended or attempted to teach. Without realizing it, he very likely would grow up believing it's the husband's job to do laundry (I'm sure his future wife will be thrilled). I wonder what other things my children have already learned about the roles of husbands and wives.

> **THE WAYS YOU TREAT AND TALK TO YOUR CHILDREN WILL SOMEDAY BE THE WAYS THEY ARE TREATING AND TALKING TO YOU.**

DON'T DISH IT OUT IF YOU CAN'T TAKE IT

As a final warning, I'd like to tell you to be careful how you act toward your children, because how you treat them is how they'll eventually treat you. Don't dish it out if you can't take it, because you'll definitely reap what you sow. The ways you treat and talk to your children will someday be the ways they will treat and talk to you. Are you ready for that? Can you take it when it's handed back to you? You would be wise to ask yourself, "What if my child turned out just like me?" How would you feel? What might you decide to change?

Here are a few points to ponder as you evaluate what your life may be saying:

1. "If children are taught to lie for parents, they are taught to lie to parents."[10]

2. Kids model everything, even their parents' self concept and self-esteem.

3. Be careful what you say when you think the kids aren't listening ... they're always listening.

4. If you want a kid who can stand up for what she believes, be a parent who knows what you believe and be willing to stand up for it.

5. Is it appropriate to interrupt a child to tell her not to interrupt?

6. If sarcasm is "joking" when it comes from you, why is it "disrespect" when it comes from your child?

7. Don't expect your child to open up and share with you if you never open up and share with her.

8. How do you teach good sportsmanship while you're running down your child's coach after a lost game?

9. How do you teach a child to say "I'm sorry" and seek forgiveness if you never admit to being wrong?

10. How do you teach a child to believe she can do anything she sets her mind to if you refuse to follow your
dreams?

Did some of these hit a little too close to home? I hope so.
I hope this chapter has inspired you to seriously evaluate
what you're teaching your child even when you aren't
actively trying to teach at all. I hope it will encourage you to
make necessary changes now that will help you feel good
about what your child is learning from your life.

Parenting in Practice

Girls/Guys Night Out

One privilege parents have is teaching our kids what it means
to be a boy or a girl. Teaching them to accept and appreciate the
special qualities and attributes they have as a result of their
gender can be fun—and a special bonding time between dads
and sons and moms and daughters. You can do this exercise
with children of about any age, but it's especially appreciated
by kids six to seven years and older. One reason is because
younger children (toddlers through about six to seven years
old) are developmentally more attached to the parent of the
opposite sex. This is where we see "Daddy's little girl" and
"Mommy's little boy." But in early school age, children begin to
become more interested in and attached to the parent of their
same sex. Girls want to learn how to be a lady, and boys want
to find out what it means to be a man. This is the perfect time
to schedule outings that bring all the girls in the family together
and others that include just the boys. You can do some really
"girly" or "manly" activities the other sex wouldn't appreciate
as much, or you can just hang out together. Either way, your
children will love being "one of the girls or guys."

CHAPTER 7

I DON'T KNOW HOW I FEEL!

Helping Your Child Understand and Express Feelings

If you think feelings are difficult to understand as an adult, just think how hard it must be for children to comprehend what's going on inside of them. Just as it's our job as parents to help our children learn to walk, talk, and read, it's also our job to help teach them to understand their feelings—not just how to label them, but also how to manage and express them appropriately.

TEACHING CHILDREN TO LABEL AND UNDERSTAND THEIR EMOTIONS

WHAT AM I FEELING AND WHY DO I FEEL THIS WAY?

Before you can teach your children about feelings, you first need to understand them yourself. Do you know how to label what you're feeling in different situations? Is your feelings vocabulary bigger than sad, mad, and glad? Are you comfortable with a wide range of emotions? These are all essential skills to help you give your child a healthy view of emotions. Not only do you need to clearly understand a wide range of emotions, you also need to know how to express them. One of the first ways a child learns about feelings is by studying how Mom and Dad express themselves.

ALTHOUGH WE CAN'T CONTROL OUR CHILDREN'S FEELINGS, WE CAN INFLUENCE HOW THEY LEARN TO EXPRESS AND LABEL THOSE FEELINGS.

You're sitting with your two-year-old son during a storm when a huge clap of thunder rattles the house. Little Joshua startles and knows something just happened because his heart skipped a beat, but he doesn't know what he's feeling or what to do with that physical sensation. So what does he do? He immediately looks to you for a signal that will tell him how to react in this situation. If you jump through the ceiling and yell, or grab him strongly and say, "I know you're scared, but it will be OK," little Joshua will learn to label thunder something to be scared of and will likely cling to you and cry.

But what if you startle right along with Joshua because the thunder took you both by surprise, but then quickly and softly say, "Wow, that thunder was loud, and really surprised me," then continue reading to him as you were before the thunder? Now, Joshua will probably take the thunder in stride, realize he, too, felt "surprised," and go back to listening to you read.

Although we can't control our children's feelings, we can influence how they learn to express and label those feelings. Consider how different parent responses could lead to different expressions from children in these situations:

- A big dog comes running up to you and your child ...
- A pet dies or runs away ...

- Your child falls and scrapes his knee ...
- Your child has a bad dream and comes running into your bedroom ...

These are all normal life events and wonderful opportunities for parents to positively influence how children understand, label, and express feelings. Your child will look to you for information about how to experience these sensations he's feeling, so it will be important that you have a healthy view of emotions and their place in our lives.

I once heard a story about a little girl who walked to and from school every day. One day, storm clouds started to form in midafternoon, and by the time school let out there was thunder and lightning. Noticing the potential danger for her daughter and concerned that she'd be scared walking home, her mother jumped in the car and headed out to pick the little girl up. She spotted her daughter on the sidewalk and noticed something strange. Every time the thunder clapped, the daughter would freeze in position, look toward the sky, and smile. This happened several times. When mom called her daughter over to the car, she asked, "What were you doing?" The little girl smiled and answered, "Smiling for God. He just keeps taking pictures of me."

> **As parents, we need to make the full range of emotions— not just happiness— acceptable.**

Now that's a positive view of storms. I don't know for sure, but I would guess this child had been taught from a very young age, through her parents' words and reactions, that storms are nothing to fear.

ALL FEELINGS ARE CREATED EQUAL

One of your first tasks will be to normalize a wide range of feelings for your child. Helping children understand that feelings are a normal and expected part of life will help. Feelings aren't good or bad; they're just feelings. They result from thoughts, behaviors, circumstances, and environments, but the feelings themselves shouldn't be judged as right or wrong. As parents, we need to make the full range of emotions—not just happiness—acceptable. We also need to describe feelings in more terms than simply sad, mad, or happy. The larger our feeling vocabulary, the better our children will learn to label what they're experiencing.

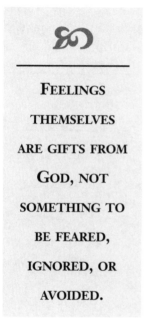

FEELINGS THEMSELVES ARE GIFTS FROM GOD, NOT SOMETHING TO BE FEARED, IGNORED, OR AVOIDED.

One of the biggest difficulties here is getting parents comfortable with the full spectrum of emotions. Realizing that God created us with our emotions may help. God gave us feelings to help us experience life. Can you imagine going through life unable to experience joy, peace, love, or excitement? But God didn't stop at what we consider the "positive" emotions. He also provided a full range of other emotions that help serve as warnings that something may be wrong or help us move through difficult times. We need to feel anger, grief, fear, disappointment, embarrassment, shock, and uncertainty sometimes as well.

It's important to note these emotions aren't reserved for one gender or the other. Girls can and do feel anger, and boys can be sad and cry. We need to learn to accept all these feelings for ourselves and each of our children.

What Parents Must Learn

The first stage in teaching children to understand and express their emotions once again is for parents to learn how to do this. As parents, we must learn to accept and be comfortable with our own feelings and the expression of a wide range of emotions if we hope to teach our children to let their feelings out. Avoid sending signals to your child that his feelings are wrong—but, at the same time, curb his expression of these feelings into appropriate behavior. If you're not comfortable with anger, sadness, or other, less-positive feelings, you won't accept even appropriate expressions of these emotions.

How do you become comfortable with the expression of uncomfortable feelings? It begins by accepting that feelings themselves are gifts from God, not something to be feared, ignored, or avoided. All our emotions serve a purpose and, when expressed within acceptable limits, can and do help us live life more fully.

Many adults I meet really do seem to believe certain emotions (especially the negative ones) are wrong. I've actually had people tell me the Bible says "do not be angry" and that anger is a sin. But as we then look at Scripture together, they soon realize they've been misquoting Scripture. The Bible doesn't say "Do not be angry." What it does say in Ephesians 4:26 is, "In your anger do not sin," followed by "Do not let the sun go down while you are still angry." Both of these statements acknowledge that anger will be experienced—it's how we manage and express anger that can become a problem.

We can take this one step further by looking at the model Jesus gave us. Jesus himself experienced a wide range of emotions, including "negative" ones. He experienced anger (Mark 3:5; John 2:14–16), grief and sadness (Matt. 26:37–38; John 11:35), and frustration (Matt. 15:16), just to name a few. Jesus also acknowledged and accepted the feelings of those around him without condemning them for having them (John 15:11; 16:6, 20, 22). If these feelings are wrong, Jesus' expression of them and acceptance of them in others would be considered sin. We all know that Jesus didn't sin nor encourage others to. But if you believe some feelings are wrong, you couldn't believe he never sinned.

BE PATIENT WITH YOUR CHILD AS HE WORKS THROUGH HIS FEELINGS, REALIZING HIS PACE MAY BE VERY DIFFERENT FROM YOURS.

Besides examining Scripture's view of negative emotions, you also may need to consider how you were allowed to express negative feelings as you were growing up. Many adults can look back on their own childhoods and see times where the expression of certain feelings (either by themselves or the adults around them) wasn't safe. They may have had a home environment where expressed anger was harmful to them, or they were punished for expressing feelings such as sadness or anger. These childhood learning experiences have a huge impact on our adult view and acceptance of emotions.

If you grew up in a home that didn't allow healthy and safe emotional expression, your childhood probably affects your comfort level with feelings in your home today. Without realizing it, you may be repeating old patterns or going to the other extreme of emotional expression (probably just as unhealthy). I encourage you to take inventory of how feelings were or weren't expressed in your home growing up. Based on what you learn, talk with your spouse and decide together how you want to teach your children to express their emotions. If you continue to struggle with being comfortable with appropriate emotional expression, you may want to seek professional counseling to help you. Don't just blindly repeat unhealthy patterns.

THREE BIG DON'TS FOR PARENTS

As you're working to teach your children to accept and understand their own feelings and express them in healthy ways, either of the following actions will undermine your efforts. Each is destructive to the parent-child relationship and may cause your child to stop feeling safe enough to express his emotions with you.

DON'T FIX IT

Parents need to learn to allow children to experience and process their own feelings. This is hard for us because we hate to see our children in pain. Also, since we're not the one swamped by the emotion, we often can think things through more quickly and rationally than our children can. So we figure out a possible solution and jump right in and try to alleviate their pain.

Moving into "fix it" mode before your child has asked for help can send him the message, "I don't believe you can handle this situation, so I'll fix it for you." This decreases a child's self-confidence in being able to manage his own life. The other message you may be sending your child is, "Those emotions don't belong here, so let's move on." Jumping into "fix it" mode tells a child he's not getting over his feeling fast enough, so you're going to help him. Neither of these messages fosters a healthy view of difficult emotions.

Even as an adult, I know how it frustrates me when I'm expressing how I feel and Jim tries to fix it. His intentions are good; he hates to see me in pain. But what it says to me is,

"You're not smart enough to solve this problem, so I'll tell you what to do." Although he was trying to help me feel better, this usually results in my feeling angry at him on top of the other feeling I already had. That's not what he was hoping for. So we've decided that when I'm experiencing strong feelings and need to vent, Jim just listens. He waits for me to get through the feelings enough so that my own rational thinking returns and I can start problem solving. He doesn't give any advice or suggestions until I say, "What do you think I should do?" That's his cue to jump in and start helping me feel better. But what he doesn't realize is he was helping me feel better long before he said a word. His being there and accepting me and my feelings is exactly what I needed.

That same process can and does work with children. Noticing their feelings, accepting them, and allowing your child whatever time he needs to process his feelings will help him know you trust him to be able to manage these emotions or ask you for help if and when he needs it. Helping kids know they're allowed to have "down days" and don't have to be happy all the time gives them the freedom not to feel rushed to get past a difficult emotion.

DON'T IGNORE IT

At the other extreme, some parents, trying to avoid "fixing it," may go too far and come across as ignoring their child's feelings altogether. Other parents may ignore their children's feelings due to their own discomfort with negative feelings. Either way, don't ignore a child's feelings. Be patient with your child as he works through his feelings, realizing his pace may be very different from yours. However, don't let your child get stuck in a feeling he can't seem to manage or allow him to wallow in his negative feelings. By staying close by, checking in on him, and asking how you can help him, you'll know if he's working through the feelings or if he's stuck and needs some encouragement.

Once he's had time to express his feelings, he'll be better able to talk about what brought on those feelings and what, if anything, needs to be done to change the situation. You may want to make yourself available by saying something like, "I'm here if you need some help with this," but then be sure to wait on him to ask you for that help.

DON'T JUDGE YOUR CHILD'S FEELINGS

"You shouldn't feel that way."
"This isn't that big a deal. Why are you so upset?"
"Do you see anyone else crying about this?"
"Oh, it didn't hurt that bad."
"It was just a toy; get over it."

Many of us have, at one time or another, said something like that to one of our children. But when you hear statements like this out of context, you realize how insensitive these comments really are to a hurting child (or anyone else).

What right do we have to tell anyone how they should feel or how bad something hurt? My friend Kathy told me about being at a local grocery store with her young nephew, who had begged to push the cart. She let him and was walking in front of him to be sure he didn't run over anyone. But then he did run over someone ... her. The cart slightly caught her ankle and she turned quickly to remind the youngster to be careful and if that happened again she'd resume pushing the cart herself.

A few minutes later, he hit her again, only harder this time. Even a slight collision on the ankle can really hurt, and my friend let out a yelp. As she turned to take control of the cart, her nephew said, "I just barely hit you. It couldn't really hurt." She responded, "Hey now, it happened to me. I should get to say how bad it hurt."

Although Kathy's ankle was in physical pain, the premise stands true for emotional pain as well. Whatever happened to your child, shouldn't he get to be the judge of how bad it hurt?

It's important to remember that feelings are just feelings. They're not right or wrong, but they are *mine*, and I should get to determine how big they are. Now, I'm not saying that some children won't be extreme in their emotional reactions or even try to use them to manipulate a parent. But wait until the feeling has passed to discuss those issues.

> **PARENTS NEED TO LEARN TO ACCEPT THAT THEIR CHILDREN'S FEELINGS MAY BE DIFFERENT FROM THEIR OWN.**

Tiara, our middle child, is very emotional. Everything seems to be a big deal to her. Her tears come frequently and often at times and levels that Jim and I think are unnecessary and out of proportion. We used to say that Tiara would give the exact same intensity of emotions to a hangnail as a broken bone. Often, we'd hear a blood-curdling scream and go running, only to find her brother had hit her over the head with a harmless blow-up bat or something of the sort.

It was difficult not to just blow off Tiara's emotional reactions (and I can't say we didn't at times). But the most effective way of managing her reactions was to let them pass, then discuss with her later what screaming like that says to a parent and that if she keeps reacting so strongly to every situation, we won't know when something really bad happens. Tiara is still very emotional, but she's beginning to show a healthier range of emotional reactions.

Finally, parents need to learn to accept that their children's feelings may be different from their own. As families go through life together, they'll experience good and bad, happy and sad times together—but everyone in the house may not feel the same way about the same circumstances. The death of a pet, a move to a new home, leaving for vacation, a major job change, all have the potential to prompt various emotions. As parents, we should remember our children have the right to their own reactions and not try to force or expect them to feel the same way we do.

TEACHING CHILDREN HOW TO EXPRESS FEELINGS

Once you understand and accept that emotions themselves aren't wrong, but a normal part of human existence, you'll be better able to teach your children how to express any and all of their emotions in a healthy and appropriate way. Right now, we'll primarily focus on the less-pleasant feelings, such as anger, sadness, hurt, frustration, and disappointment. We all seem to do fairly well with the expression of positive emotions; it's the negative ones we struggle with, so that's what we'll address.

> ### HEALTHY EMOTIONAL EXPRESSION BEGINS WITH BEING GIVEN PERMISSION TO LET IT OUT.

GIVE KIDS PERMISSION TO EXPRESS HOW THEY FEEL

Although the first step is to help kids understand and learn to label what they are feeling, that alone isn't enough. "OK, so I can tell you what I'm feeling, but what am I supposed to *do* with this feeling?" they may ask. Kids don't automatically know how to get feelings out, and they sure don't know how to do it appropriately.

Since babies come out crying and screaming and keep it up more than we'd like, we may be led to believe they're born knowing how to express emotions, but that's not true. Babies use crying to communicate everything they need, want, and feel, but as children grow and they learn to express themselves in other ways, crying decreases. They're looking for more specific and clear ways to express what they need and feel. It's our job to help with that.

Healthy emotional expression begins with being given permission to let it out. All of us have watched a child experience something difficult and try to hold back the feelings. As a parent, you can read between the lines and know your child's holding something in by his body language and non-verbal communication. When you see these signals, just saying it's OK to feel may be all it takes.

A few months ago our youngest child, Talon, had to have an MRI. Since he was only five, he was sedated for the procedure. (I guess the hospital staff didn't think an active five-year-old could lie "perfectly still"—imagine that.) As much as Jim and I hated this, we knew it had to be done and talked openly to Talon about what to expect. Between us and the wonderful nursing staff, he was as prepared as he could possibly be, but that didn't stop his anxiety and certainly didn't stop the pain of the needles (especially when the IV took more than one try).

I held Talon while the IV was being placed, and all I remember is his body tensing up and a slight whimper. He was such a trooper, and everyone in the room told him so. But as we headed back to his room to wait for the next step, I noticed he wasn't talking. He would nod or shake his head when Jim or I talked to him, but that was about all. His body was still tense, and every once in a while we'd see his lip begin to quiver. Parents need to be tuned in to such non-verbal signals.

Once we were back in his room, I sat beside him on the bed, hugged him, and said, "Talon, it's OK to cry and let it out." And out it came! "Whaaaaaaa!" at the top of his lungs. As I sat there holding him, I remember thinking, "How long would he have kept that inside if I hadn't given him permission to cry?" I don't really understand why it didn't come out naturally, but I learned that some kids need more help than others to express what they're feeling. Take time to study your children and know their signals. If you notice something being held back, just take a minute and give permission to let it out.

GIVE THEM ALTERNATIVES

As you look at little Jared, you notice that he is getting really upset. You can see the emotions building, and he just can't seem to get it under control; it's like the feelings are bigger than he is. That's probably closer to the truth than you may know. Emotions (especially the negative ones) are big and need to have some sort of outlet. Unfortunately, we as parents often fail in this area. We're really good at telling children what *not* to do:

> "Stop that!"
> "Don't give me that look."
> "Don't talk to me that way."
> "Don't slam the door."

But how good are we at giving them something they *can* do when their feelings are getting bigger than they are? The steam won't evaporate just because we haven't taught our children appropriate and acceptable ways to let it off. Instead, it will keep building until the child finds any means at all to release it—including hitting his little sister, yelling at a friend, or kicking the dog. If you continue to avoid teaching your kids proper ways to express these negative feelings, by the time they're sixteen, they'll have developed an entire arsenal of destructive expressions.

ACTIVELY DIRECT THE CHILD TO THINGS HE CAN *DO* TO RELEASE THE ENERGY BURST THAT COMES WITH EMOTIONS LIKE ANGER AND FRUSTRATION.

Managing negative emotions requires active parental teaching. This is no time to sit back and see what little Jared can come up with on his own. Instead, intervene and actively direct that child to things he can *do* to release the energy burst that comes with emotions like anger and frustration. Many parents say, "When Jared is mad, I want him just to talk calmly to me about these feelings." Yeah, right! Can you do that? Probably not until you have time to cool down. Kids need to learn ways to get the anger energy out so they *can* cool off enough to talk about what's happening.

Teaching children that even intense emotions can be expressed appropriately begins with how you deal with both your own negative emotions and theirs. They're learning what's acceptable in your home by how you express negative feelings. Yelling at Jared to "stop yelling!" simply tells Jared yelling is allowed.

You may not like it when he imitates you, but you have to realize what you're teaching. He notices you head straight to the cookie jar when you're discouraged and to the mall when you're lonely. He sees you throw the hammer across the driveway when you get frustrated and grab a beer when you're anxious.

If you want Jared to express his feelings in healthy, constructive, and non-self-defeating ways, you must learn to do the same yourself. Once you have your emotional expressions within a healthy range, you can model and teach these to your children.

Then you can direct your child to appropriate ways to let out the energy burst that comes with feelings. Remember, these emotions are big, so the outlets must be bigger than "sit down and tell me how you feel."

You and your spouse will need to talk through what type of physical expressions you're each comfortable with, then start discussing them with your children. (The Parenting in Practice section at the end of this chapter will help you.) When a feeling hits, you'll likely have to remind them of things they can do to get the energy out. Simply saying, "Jared, you look really mad. Why don't you go hammer some nails for a few minutes?" can help him feel you accept his feelings and want to help him express them in healthy ways. Be sure to top it off with praise when he has expressed and managed his negative feelings in an effective and proper manner.

PARENTING IN PRACTICE

To begin teaching your kids appropriate ways to express their emotions, come up with a list of several alternatives that you and your spouse can be comfortable with in your home. It may be easier to first come up with expressions that make you uncomfortable—things you've already heard yourself telling your child not to do. Then, realizing that your children need guidance in coming up with ways they can express their feelings, work together to brainstorm outlets for emotions (especially the negative ones that seem most difficult to express appropriately).

Physical outlets that don't cause harm or destruction are a good way to start. Letting a child use his body to express how big the feeling is will actually help him be able to talk it through later. Once the two of you agree on a list of several alternatives, discuss these with your kids and be willing to remind them to use these healthier outlets when the need arises. Some suggestions:

- Batting cage
- Punching bag
- Running hard around the house or yard
- Screaming as loud as he can (outside)
- Hammering nails into a board
- Chopping wood
- Stomping his feet
- Slamming a door
- Kicking a coffee can half full of rocks around the garage
- Throwing a rubber ball against the side of the house
- Tearing up an old phone book
- Beating up his bed and pillows

It's up to you to decide what's acceptable in your home. Not everyone will be comfortable with the same things, but you need to allow your children some physical outlets for their feelings that you deem appropriate.

CHAPTER 8

CHILDREN OF VIRTUE

The Art of Instilling Values into Your Children

On January 17, 2005, news outlets all over the country were telling the story of twelve-year-old Andrew Gieseler from Naperville, Illinois, who overnight became something of a role model. On a routine trip to a local Target store to buy sneakers, Andrew encountered a moral decision. He and his mother and younger brother were entering the store when Andrew found a clear plastic bag stuffed full with $9,000 laying on a deserted stretch of sidewalk. When his mother asked what he thought he should do with his find, Andrew was reported to have replied immediately, "We should bring it inside." They promptly did.

Although the money didn't belong to Target, the manager and Andrew's mother both expressed how proud they were of Andrew, his sense of what was right, and his handling of the situation. His mother was quoted saying, "I was impressed he knew what to do and did it without any question. It was interesting because Andrew and I had been having a conversation on the way to Target about honesty." During a later interview, Andrew said he hadn't even thought of keeping the money. "It would leave a tarnish on your conscience the rest of your life," he said.

Isn't it great to hear true stories of kids who demonstrate strong morals? In this case, it was obvious Andrew's mother had been talking and teaching about honesty before the situation even came up. Anyone would have been proud to be Andrew's parent at that time. We all hope we're raising our children to become responsible and respectable adults.

> **YOUR CHILD WILL BEGIN TO GROW IN HER UNDERSTANDING OF WHAT'S EXPECTED OF HER BY BEING IMMERSED IN A VIRTUOUS LIFESTYLE.**

However, instilling strong values and morals into our kids doesn't come easily, quickly, or naturally. Children aren't born with the knowledge or even desire to be "good kids." All through Scripture, there are references to the "fleshly nature" we're born with and how, since the fall of man, its desires are evil (Eph. 2:3; 2 Tim. 2:22; James 1:14–15 just to mention a few). We're all born with natural desires that aren't conducive to living a good life.

Knowing that, we as parents have our jobs cut out for us if we hope to impart virtues to our children that will govern them instead of their natural desires. It's said that leaving a child to her own devices to grow a strong moral foundation would be like leaving the garden to decide for itself what it's going to grow. A garden left to its own devices grows mainly one thing: weeds. If you don't want your child growing weeds as her belief system, you'd better get involved.

This will demand parents' active participation for as many years as you have contact with your kids. Ruth

Wilson, PhD, says caring and moral character "doesn't develop or exist in isolation. For children to learn to be caring individuals requires the attentions and involvement of the significant adults in their lives…. For children to develop the virtue of caring, they need to be immersed in a way of living and learning which expresses, or reflects, an attitude of caring."[11]

As children grow and mature, they become better able to understand the concept and importance of values, but you don't want to wait until they can fully comprehend these issues to start teaching. You will need to start teaching the concepts of honesty, respect, gratitude, servanthood, and other virtues even before your children can really understand the concepts. Your child will begin to grow in her understanding of what's expected of her by being immersed in a virtuous lifestyle, consistently exposed and introduced to moral concepts.

At the risk of sounding redundant, I'll reiterate that your most powerful tool is how you choose to live your own life. If you model high moral and ethical standards, that will teach your children the most about values and how they guide your life. Words are important, and talking about moral issues is also essential in developing strong values in your child. But no amount of words will override, make up for, or counter the model you set through your own lifestyle. Work hard to be sure you're living the type of life you hope

IF WE WANT OUR CHILDREN TO DEVELOP A HEALTHY SENSE OF MORALITY, WE MUST LEAD THEM TO GOD AS THEIR SPIRITUAL AND MORAL FOUNDATION.

your child will imitate. Ask yourself regularly, "What did my child learn today by watching me?"

SO WHERE DO WE BEGIN?

The first step is determining exactly which values you hope to teach. There's a long list of virtues that govern healthy living and relationships, and all of them are important. Even Scripture is full of hundreds of dos and don'ts that help us live a righteous and respectable life, but we'd become overwhelmed quickly if we thought we had to teach each and every one of them. However, I believe God already made this task more manageable. Just by looking at three sections of Scripture, we can get a quick view of just what we want our kids to learn.

THE GREATEST COMMANDMENT

> Teacher, which is the greatest commandment in the Law?
>
> Jesus replied: "Love the Lord your God with all your heart and with all your soul and with all your mind." This is the first and greatest commandment. And the second is like it: "Love your neighbor as yourself." All the Law and the Prophets hang on these two commandments. (Matt. 22:36–40)

Jesus himself says that these two commandments sum up all the law. The law was the written code of conduct used to govern how people lived. It included the Ten Commandments and much more (some of which were more rules than moral guidelines). The law was what parents were instructed to teach their children and to live by themselves.

Jesus summed it all up in two concepts. First, love God with everything in you. As we love God and give our lives to him, we'll want to live according to his principles instead of our evil desires. If we want our children to develop a healthy sense of morality, we must lead them to God as their spiritual and moral foundation. Without this relationship, we won't have the strength to overcome our fleshly desires.

The second greatest commandment is to love your neighbor as yourself. Be sure to look at that little, two-letter word "as" in that verse. Moral development is not only about how you treat others, but also about how you treat yourself. Understanding that you're a valuable person worthy of respect will help you understand that every other person deserves the same.

THE GOLDEN RULE

So, if the greatest commandment is the foundation of values and virtues, the next two sections are the action behind the theory. Putting a theory into real-life action is often difficult. But once again, God provides the directions. In one short verse, he gives the foundation for teaching, training, and modeling good morals to our children.

Matthew 7:12 says, "So in everything, do to others what you would have them do to you, for this sums up the Law and the Prophets." Again Jesus says that he has summed up the law for us. He understood we could get bogged down with all the laws' specifics, so, like any good teacher, he decided to make it easier for us.

AN ATTITUDE OF GRATITUDE BEGINS WITH A CONTENT HEART.

Helping children identify how they'd like others to treat them is one way of teaching them how they should treat others. This is especially hard for young children, who are naturally selfish and egocentric. But as we consistently expose them to this concept, it begins to take shape. They become better able to see things from others' perspectives, to realize how their actions impact others and to work to treat others the way they want to be treated.

THE LOVE CHAPTER

First Corinthians 13—known as the love chapter—gives us insight into putting action behind our values. Verses 4–7 give some very specific attributes and actions that govern a healthy and moral lifestyle: *"Love is* patient, *love is* kind. *It* does not envy, *it* does not boast, *it is* not proud. *It is* not rude, *it is* not self-seeking, *it is* not easily angered, *it* keeps no record of wrongs. *Love does not delight in evil* but rejoices with the truth. *It always* protects, *always* trusts, *always* hopes, *always* perseveres."* Well, there's a list of virtues if I ever saw one:

- Patience
- Kindness
- Contentment and gratitude (does not envy)
- Humility (does not boast, is not proud)
- Respectfulness (is not rude)
- Servanthood (is not self-seeking, always protects)
- Tolerance (not easily angered)
- Forgiveness (no record of wrongs)
- Honesty (rejoices with the truth)
- Trustworthiness
- Optimism (always hopes)
- Perseverance

It's beyond this book's scope to examine all these virtues, but I'll address a couple that I hear parents concerned about most in their children—gratitude and respect.

GRATITUDE

Instilling an attitude of gratitude in our children seems to be getting more and more difficult. Our society is constantly bombarding us with materialism and the need for more of everything. I often hear parents say they feel they're fighting a losing battle in the area of gratitude. "No matter what I do or how much I give, it just never seems to be enough."

I guess that's kind of like trying to fill up a hole by digging it deeper. You aren't going to teach your child gratefulness for what she has as long as you continue to give her more. Part of the problem is that we as parents have bought into society's "more is better" attitude—then we wonder why our children have caught the same disease.

An attitude of gratitude begins with a contented heart. Teaching our children that everything we have comes from God and that we are to be grateful for our many blessings is a good first step. When we really realize we don't deserve any of this stuff and that even the poorest American would be considered wealthy by much of the rest of the world, we may begin to form a more accurate perspective.

I often teach people of all ages to figure out who they are comparing themselves to (we all do this whether we want to admit it or not). Discontentment grows out of always comparing your health, wealth, talents, and friends to people who have more than you. Wherever you fall in the pecking order, you can always find someone out there who has more. When you're looking into their lives, your heart will always be yearning for more and will be discontent, selfish, and self-absorbed.

On the other hand, determining who you will compare yourself to can also foster an attitude of contentment and gratefulness. Just as you can always find someone who has more than you, you can also always find someone who has less. Comparing what you have to people who are living a life with much less will definitely begin to change your perspective.

You can help your child understand how very blessed she really is by regularly exposing her to people who have less. Volunteering at a homeless shelter, studying missions and people of other cultures, donating clothes and toys to a family who lost everything in a fire, adopting a less-fortunate family during the holidays, or buying groceries for a family who just lost a job are just a few ways to keep your child focused on those who have less instead of those who have more.

> YOU CAN HELP YOUR CHILD UNDERSTAND HOW VERY BLESSED SHE REALLY IS BY REGULARLY EXPOSING HER TO PEOPLE WHO HAVE LESS.

Changing your child's focus is only part of the equation for creating gratitude. You as a parent need to stop modeling the more-is-better attitude. Stop believing that you and your child need the biggest and best the world has to offer to be happy. I'm not saying having nice things is wrong—but these things become wrong when they become our major focus. If your child has to have the latest fashion from the hottest store or life is going to fall apart, there's a problem.

Let me share stories about two different people with you. The first is a young, unmarried, pregnant girl we'll call Miranda. Miranda is twenty years old and comes from a divorced family. Neither of her parents ever had much money, but they provided for her as best they could. As soon as she was old enough, she got a job and used her money to buy "all the things I never had." What that really meant was "clothes with a label I never had." She always had clean, fashionable clothes growing up, but they didn't come from the hottest stores or have the most popular logo running across them, and that was what she was after. She tried living on her own for a while, but couldn't manage the finances due to her "need" for the best stuff. She eventually moved back home.

When I met Miranda, she was still living at home and saying how much she hated it. She had found a boyfriend and was thinking about moving in with him, but when she found out she was pregnant, he dropped her. She felt her life was in shambles, and she didn't know how she was going to raise this baby on such a tight budget. Then she told me how her mother and aunt had gone to garage sales and bought several things for the baby. She shared this with an attitude of disgust and embarrassment and said that she couldn't believe they'd do that. "My baby will not wear hand-me-downs or garage-sale clothes!" All I could think was, "Oh, how very sad."

Let me compare that with another family. I don't know their names, but they made a huge impression on me. A few years ago, Jim and I had a garage sale. We each went through our closets and tried to weed out the clothes that we would never wear again. Jim found several very nice suits he'd long since outgrown and decided it was time to part with them. We both knew adult clothes never sell well at garage sales, so we decided we'd probably donate these to a local clothing bank, but we put them out just in case.

About midmorning, a lady came by and was looking at the clothes, especially the suits Jim had put out. She said she had a thirteen-year-old son who really needed a suit, and she thought these just might fit him. She asked if she could bring him by later that day to try them on. I said, "Of course," but I was thinking, "Do you really think a thirteen-year-old boy is going to be happy with a garage-sale suit?"

A few hours later, the lady and her son returned. He was a handsome young man with a smile plastered across his face.

When his mom showed him the suits he lit up and said, "Those are great! Do you think they'll fit?" He tried each one on and came out of the house to show his mom how they fit. He smiled the entire time and talked excitedly about how much he liked the suits. After trying them on and considering the minor alterations that would be needed, his mother told him that they could afford just one. He immediately responded with a huge hug and thank-you to his mom and went to choose which one he wanted. This young man's attitude of gratitude so touched me that I handed his mother all the suits that were there and told her they were hers—no charge. That mother and son demonstrated more gratitude than I think I'd ever seen. And as they left, I knew I would never forget them.

CHILDREN NEED TO LEARN EARLY ON THAT THE WORLD DOESN'T REVOLVE AROUND THEM.

These two stories show how powerful a mindset of contentment and appreciation can be. Are you and your children thankful for what you have? Are you content? Do you consider whatever you receive a blessing, or are you picky and ungrateful? Your children are watching and learning about gratefulness from you and your attitudes toward material possessions.

RESPECT

As I said before, respect is hard to define and can be a difficult concept to teach our children. But as they watch us treat others (including them) in ways we describe as respectful, they'll begin to catch on. Look at the virtue of respectfulness from two angles: First, you want to teach kids to respect themselves; second, you want to teach them to respect others.

Instilling self-respect means helping your child understand she's a valuable person, and her thoughts, opinions, and feelings matter. It involves helping her think through moral and ethical issues and work to develop her own standards of who she wants to be and what she believes, not just mimic Mom and Dad. Of course, we hope our children will adopt a similar stand on major moral issues and how they choose to live their lives, but it's not our job to force that. If we "walk the talk," discuss openly with our children why we've chosen the path we have, and begin instilling these character traits from a very young age through the way we parent them, they'll likely surprise you by how closely their standards match yours. But by the time your child is a teen, telling her how she "must" or "should" believe or behave could shoot her in the other direction. Trust her to think through situations that come her way and to use the foundation you've laid to make strong moral choices.

When your child feels she has chosen for herself how she wants to live and treat other people, she's much more likely to stand strong in those convictions. When she can describe why she believes premarital sex is wrong beyond "because my parents said so," she will have internalized this conviction and will hold it closer to her heart.

Help your child get to this point by opening up conversations about moral topics and asking her what she thinks and why. Don't offer your reasoning until you have completely heard her out. Don't interrupt when she says, "I'm not sure what I believe about that." A stern, "What do you mean you don't know? There is only one answer to that question," won't help her keep the topic open to process her thoughts in a safe environment—and it's definitely not modeling respect for her opinions.

Showing respect for others is the other side of the respectfulness coin. Children need to learn early on that the world doesn't revolve around them and that everyone on earth is created equal and deserves to be treated as such. A virtuous person shows respect by treating others as they themselves would want to be treated, and this puts many of the other virtues into action.

ℰℐ

DEVELOPING GOOD COMMUNICATION SKILLS IS FUNDAMENTAL.

Being respectful of others means being tolerant of differences, seeing others as equal to you, treating them with patience and kindness, and being willing to put their needs before your own. You'll teach this concept daily as you interact with the world around you. Are you patient with the new cashier at the grocery store? Are you considerate of your child's feelings when weekend plans have to change? Do you treat people of different races, religions, and regions the same as those who are more similar to you? Do you resolve conflicts with your spouse peaceably? Do you stand firm for what you believe? Does she know what your convictions are and how you stand on important moral issues? Consider these things as you work to teach your child to respect herself and the world around her.

PARENTING IN PRACTICE

HAVE A DATE WITH YOUR CHILD

Date time is special one-on-one time you get to spend with your child. I suggest you let your child help plan these special outings. You may have to set some boundaries, but this helps you learn what activities your child enjoys.

Both time and money are concerns for most of us, but

there are ways to get around those problems and still have date time. No excuse is good enough to keep you from one-on-one time with your kids. It must be a priority. Notice that I say, "have a date" not "go on a date." You can learn to date without ever leaving your house or without spending any (or much) money. I've worked with many families who were struggling financially. They still learned to have periodic dates with their kids—they just became very creative planning the activities.

The following list includes possible dates for even the smallest pocketbooks to get you started. Use it to help you brainstorm dates. Once you begin scheduling regular dates with your children, you'll find you both look forward to these special times.

1. Bake cookies together.
2. Play a board game or other game for two.
3. Go on a bike ride.
4. Roast marshmallows and make s'mores.
5. Go out to breakfast together.
6. Go to a park or playground and play on the equipment.
7. Go on a picnic.
8. Plant flowers.
9. Go to a parade.
10. Go to a circus or carnival.
11. Have an overnight girls or boys night out at a hotel and swim in the pool.
12. Go fishing.
13. Go stargazing, watch for falling stars, and make a wish together.
14. Go camping.
15. Volunteer at a local community function together.

CHAPTER 9

DO YOU HEAR WHAT I HEAR?

Learning to Communicate with Your Child

ॐ

HOW TO LISTEN SO YOUR CHILD WILL TALK

In my office, I've heard child after child say things like, "He just doesn't listen to me!" or "She doesn't understand where I'm coming from," or "I feel totally ignored when I try to talk to them." Any guesses as to whom these children are referring?

Comments like these from children indicate that major principles of communication have broken down and the relationship between them and their parents is being damaged. Communication skills are key to any relationship, and they're essential in a parent-child relationship. How you communicate can either strengthen the bond between you and your kids or drive a wedge between you, potentially causing irreparable damage. Developing good communication skills is fundamental to keeping an open, healthy, strong relationship with your children.

THE MOST IMPORTANT PART

What do you think is the most important aspect of communication? The key concept powerful enough to make or break any relationship simply by its presence or absence, so essential that without it nothing else would matter, is *listening*.

Being a good listener is the foundation and most crucial level of healthy communication in all relationships. If we want our children to talk to us, we must learn to listen *first* and *most*—then everything else will begin to fall into place. James 1:19 drives this point home: "Everyone should be quick to listen, slow to speak."

BEING A GOOD LISTENER IS THE FOUNDATION AND MOST CRUCIAL LEVEL OF HEALTHY COMMUNICATION IN ALL RELATIONSHIPS.

Listening shows you treasure your child and want to know what he thinks and feels. It's a great way to show him through your actions that he's important and you respect him and what he has to say. When you're really listening to your child, you've chosen to put yourself and your thoughts, feelings, and ideas on the back burner so you can hear him. What a great message to send your child!

If, instead, you're the type of parent who likes to hear yourself talk, you're probably not feeling very close to your kids. Although there may be a time and place for monologues in the parenting relationship, the time is very limited and the place is only with younger children. Once a child has developed his own thoughts, he'll get bored quickly by one-sided conversations and lectures and tune them out. The longer one-sided conversations go on, the more likely children will feel what they have to say is unimportant to us. Before long, they're very likely to stop talking to us all together.

"Why waste my time? He doesn't care what I think anyway."

"Why should I tell her how I feel? She always seems to think she knows better than I do."

These feelings can be the kiss of death to open parent-child communication. If you stop a conversation short by interrupting your child to interject your thoughts or feelings or to solve the problem he's describing, your actions may be telling him what he has to say is unimportant to you. Do you cause your child to think twice before sharing with you because of your tendency to judge, minimize, or invalidate what he's going through? Let me give you a better understanding of what you may be doing that stops conversations short and how to replace those behaviors with responses that will draw your child out and bring the two of you closer.

THE KEY THAT UNLOCKS THE TREASURE
OF HEALTHY CONVERSATION

Webster's Dictionary says conversation is "the verbal exchange of ideas, sentiments, or observations."[12] It's impossible to have an "exchange" with only one person involved in the conversation—or if both people are playing the same role. Just as in a gift exchange there must be a giver and a receiver. If both people in a conversation decide to talk, it will be difficult for either to receive what the other is saying. And if both people decide to listen, there would be nothing to receive. Healthy communication requires a balance of talking and listening.

LISTENING MAKES TRUE CONVERSATIONS HAPPEN AND GROWS TRUST AND INTIMACY IN THE RELATIONSHIP.

Listening is the key to unlocking the buried treasure of thoughts, feelings, and ideas that lies deep inside your child. As you take time to listen closely, your child will begin to open up and reveal to you what he holds deep inside. Listening makes true conversations happen and grows trust and intimacy in the relationship.

"I just need someone to listen to me."

All of us are looking for someone to listen to us. We want to know someone really cares what we think and is willing to stop talking to hear us.

I see the power of listening every day in my office; my profession is built on the ability to be a good listener. I've spent many therapeutic hours in silence, often with teens whose parents informed me would probably just sit there and not say a word. When the parents come back in for their session, they seem shocked their child talked at all. They often ask what I did to get their son to tell me why he's failing algebra or to encourage their daughter to tell me how she's scared about going off to college. The answer is almost always, "I just listened to him (her)."

EFFECTIVE LISTENING REQUIRES ATTENTION.

Please note that listening isn't a passive activity; it requires full concentration and active involvement. Although the *concept* of listening is quite simple (shut your mouth and open your ears), the *act* of listening isn't as simple. Effective listening requires attention. When these kids are in my office, I'm not looking at a magazine, filing my nails, or watching TV while they're trying to tell me what's on their hearts and minds. I'm looking them in the eyes and making sure they know by my body language and questions that I'm truly interested in what they have to say.

This isn't a magical formula you have to go to school for nine years to learn. Each one of us has the ability to get our children to open up and talk if we just take time to give them our full attention.

Suggestions for Being a Better Listener

Make yourself available. Set aside a few minutes every day to check in with each child individually—whether at breakfast, after school, or at bedtime doesn't really matter. What matters is your children know you want to take time to communicate with them. Don't rush through this time. Be patient and let the conversation develop.

Although this scheduled time is good, it probably won't be enough. Be aware of other times during the day or week your child may need or want to talk to you. When you notice this, stop what you're doing and make yourself available. These spontaneous conversations may give you more insight to your child's world than the scheduled ones.

Kids really feel you're listening when you're on equal footing and at eye level.

Listen with your whole body. Communication experts believe we communicate more through our body language (55%) than through our words (7%) or our tone of voice (38%).[13] So, if you want your child to really know you're listening to him, you need to communicate that with your eyes and body. This proves you're really listening so you never have to say, "Yes, I *am* listening to you." Your child will already know that you are. Make good eye contact, lean toward him, nod, and give brief interjections to show that you are listening actively.

A great *Family Circus* cartoon shows the little girl look up at her father, who's reading a newspaper, and say, "Daddy, you have to listen to me with your eyes as well as your ears." Get the picture?

Avoid distractions. To be an effective listener, you need to be able to concentrate on what your child is saying. You can't do that very well in a room full of distractions. At conversation time, turn off the TV, put down the newspaper, stop cooking dinner, and turn your attention to your children. It is practically impossible to concentrate on what someone is saying with only part of your brain working on it.

Get on their level. This is especially important when your children are little and much shorter than you are. There's a big difference between having the person you're talking to looking down at you or having that person sit or squat down to be right on your level. Kids really feel you're listening when you're on equal footing and at eye level.

Ask open-ended questions. Parents often complain that their children won't talk to them—but perhaps the reason is because the children don't believe their parents want them to. If you ask your child how school was today, you may get a one- or two-word answer until they find out if you *really* want to know.

When we greet a friend or coworker with "How are you doing?" we expect to hear, "Fine." That's considered an OK response from an adult, but we get upset when our kids answer the same way. It's because we usually really don't care how someone we're passing in the hall is doing, but it's the polite thing to ask. When we really do want to know, we take a minute and look that friend in the eye and ask again or in a slightly different way. "No, really ... how are you doing?" or maybe, "Is everything going OK at home?" Do the same with your child.

In the Cherry home, the younger the child, the more open they seem to be sharing about their day at school. As I'm writing this book, our youngest, Talon, is in kindergarten and loving it. When I ask, "How was school today?"

I'd better be ready to sit down and hear all about the fun things he did, with whom he played, and what's going on the whole next week.

But if I ask either Tiara (fourth grade) or Taffeta (seventh grade) how school was, I'll get a quick "fine" or "good" as they walk on through the room. Since I really do want to know more about their day than that, I've learned to follow up the first question with something like, "Tell me something exciting or different that happened today." When I do that, they each seem to realize I really do want to know what's going on, and the words begin to flow.

ECHOING INVOLVES ACTIVELY FOCUSING YOUR ATTENTION ON WHAT YOUR CHILD IS SAYING.

PUTTING IT ALL TOGETHER

Now that you know basic listening concepts, how do you apply these to conversations with your child? A technique I call ECHO conversation combines all the listening concepts in one conversation that results in understanding each. This process may seem awkward at first and will require some practice, but as you use it in conversations with your children, you'll soon see them modeling the same concepts back to you, even if they don't realize they're doing it.

The ECHO skills aren't necessary for general communication throughout the day, but are best used in deeper, more emotional conversations in which someone needs to feel heard and understood. The technique may be used when only one person needs time to express how he or she feels, or when a situation needs to be addressed or a problem resolved.

ECHO C ONVERSATION

Most people have stood at the entrance of a cave or the bottom of a canyon and yelled out some word or phrase, hoping to hear the words echoed back. But can you imagine yelling, "I love you," and a moment later the cave echoes, "Who cares?" or "Yeah, sure you do." Yet, conversations with our children often become that distorted.

The ECHO conversation technique combines all the necessary elements of listening in such a way that your child will know for sure you understood what he was trying to say. ECHOing involves actively focusing your attention on what your child is saying, including verbal and nonverbal information, then reflecting or "echoing" what you heard back to him.

How It Works

Let's break ECHOing into four parts to help you understand how it works in conversation.

E—E STABLISH AND E XPLAIN

The first step in ECHOing is to establish the topic. Either you or your child need to define the issue to be discussed and pick a time to sit down and talk (e.g., "Mom, I really need to talk to you about something that happened at school today. Could we make some time around eight o'clock tonight?").

Identify one of you as the speaker; the other, of course, is the listener. If your child is the first speaker, it's his job to explain his thoughts and feelings about the established topic as concisely as possible, or at least in small enough chunks for the listener to be able to remember the main points and repeat them back. You can encourage your child to pause periodically so you can reflect back to him what you believe he is expressing.

C—CONCENTRATE

As your child is talking, your job as the listener is to listen! Stop talking, and concentrate on what your child is saying and on how it's being said. Focus your attention on the words and ideas, but be sure not to miss the attitudes and feelings also being expressed through body language, tone of voice, gestures, and facial expressions. These nonverbal aspects of communication often will give you an accurate indication of his attitude and emotional state, regardless of the words being said.

While listening and concentrating, be careful not to interrupt either verbally or mentally. This is very important. Interrupting is probably the most destructive element to communication. Give your child time to say what he has to say; any questions you have may be addressed if you're patient. Interrupting shows disrespect for your child and may also show your conclusions are wrong. Waiting and listening will keep you from putting your foot in your mouth or starting an argument. Even more important, it shows you value what your child is saying more than what you may need or want to say.

Avoid distractions and choose the right time to hold an important conversation. Don't try to have an important conversation right before your family's favorite TV program or if you're expecting an important call or fixing dinner.

Parents of multiple children seem to be especially affected in this area. It seems inevitable that when one of our children *needs* to talk to us, the whole gang wants something at the exact same time. Many mothers become quite good at hearing and even responding to multiple conversations simultaneously. Responding, however, isn't listening, so, unless the topic is vitally important and can't be delayed, avoid times you know will be packed with distractions.

H—HIGHLIGHT THE MAIN POINTS

Just as in the cave, once the speaker finishes there's a brief pause, then the echo. When your child finishes speaking, take a moment to consider what you've heard, then echo it to him. However, unlike in the cave, the words reflected back may not be exactly what was spoken. The echo should summarize the main points your child presented, plus any emotional undertones or cues that may have influenced the meaning of the words. It's important to remember this is *not* the place or time for you to add in your own personal thoughts, opinions, judgments, or rebuttals. There may be time for that later; if not, maybe that's not the most important part of this particular conversation.

Let's say your son is sitting with arms and legs crossed, turned away from you. In a rough, loud voice, with an angry scowl on his face, he says, "No! I'm not angry!" If you respond, "What I heard you say is that you're not angry. Is that what you meant to say?" you wouldn't be using the ECHO conversation skills. But the ECHO response would be, "What I heard you say is that you're angry but you don't want to talk about it right now. Is that what you meant to say?" ECHOing takes into account all you see, hear, and sense to come to a conclusion.

Sometimes you'll sound like you're repeating exactly what you heard. That's OK. Actually, the more open and honest the speaker, the less interpreting the listener will have to do, and the clearer the "echo" will be.

O—OBTAIN AGREEMENT/UNDERSTANDING

The final step in ECHO conversation is the listener obtaining agreement from the speaker that he or she has heard and understood completely what the speaker was trying to say. This agreement must be reached *before* giving the listener a turn to discuss the established topic or end the conversation.

Your child says what he needs to say, followed by you ECHOing back what you heard without interjecting your own ideas or judgments. When you feel you've reflected what you heard, ask your child, "Is that what you meant to say?" If your child agrees that you did in fact hear what he was trying to say, then the conversation can be over or can flip, allowing you to share your thoughts on the topic. But if at this point your child feels that his message didn't get communicated the way he wanted it to, give him a chance to revise or restate what he was trying to say.

It's important to note that a "no" response to "Is that what you meant to say?" doesn't mean anyone messed up in the communication. It simply means we need to keep going until we both hear and understand what the speaker is trying to communicate. This process should continue until the speaker feels he or she has been completely heard and says so to, "Is that what you meant to say?"

BOTH MAY HAVE A CHANCE TO SPEAK

Many conversations involve only your child needing to share a thought or feeling about something personal. In those cases, the ECHOing is complete when that speaker feels heard and understood completely.

However, other conversations will require that both of you have the chance to express yourselves. When that's the case, you simply take turns being speaker or listener. The first speaker stays in that role until all four ECHO steps are completed. Then the second speaker should address the original issue as if he or she had been the *first* one to speak. He or she should share his or her original thoughts and feelings about the topic, instead of responding to what the other person just said. There will be time for that later. If the original thoughts and feelings aren't shared, the second speaker may never feel his or her ideas have been heard and considered.

KNOWING WHAT TO AVOID

If you truly want to understand your child better, you'll need to learn how to get him to talk to you and how to nourish that conversation once it begins. Often, instead of nourishing a conversation, we end up choking it. Both our verbal and nonverbal responses can either keep them talking or shut them up. Although we may say we want to keep them talking, our responses often do just the opposite.

Responses that can choke and eventually kill a conversation include things like telling your child how to fix a problem, criticizing or blaming him, lecturing or preaching, or giving orders. Using nonverbal responses such as closed body position, not making eye contact, or speaking in an angry or uninterested tone of voice can also shut down a conversation before it gets started.

These are things *not* to do or say. Now for some positive actions that can breathe life into a conversation.

HOW TO NOURISH A CONVERSATION

You've probably been in a conversation that seemed to die out before it even got started. On the other hand, maybe you walked away from talking to someone thinking, "Wow, I think I could have talked to her for hours and told her anything." What's the difference? Most likely, that person's verbal and nonverbal communications made the difference. Let's look at ways you can help your child feel he could talk to you for hours and tell you anything.

KEEP THEM TALKING

Use door-openers. These are open, noncoercive invitations to talk. Often you can tell by the way your child is acting that he might want to talk but is reluctant. You want him to talk, but you don't want to force him to talk. Open the door and make yourself available by inviting him to talk to you. Taking the first step by showing interest can make it easier for him to share what's on his mind.

Some examples of door-openers are: "Would you like to talk?" "I'm here if you want someone to talk to," "I sense something might be bothering you," and "I'd like to know what you think."

Demonstrate open and attentive body posture. The nonverbal communication of body posture can be very powerful, and people notice it whether we realize it or not. You communicate interest and attentiveness by facing the person who's speaking, leaning slightly forward, and keeping your arms open. You can communicate nonacceptance and a lack of interest by turning your body away (even slightly), leaning back, and crossing your arms.

Make good eye contact. Positioning yourself so you can make good eye contact and then doing it shows interest and will help keep your child talking. The amount of eye contact should be comfortable and appropriate; if it's constant or intense you may communicate you're being disapproving, critical, or judgmental. However, little or no eye contact may communicate lack of interest.

Use occasional encouragers. If you want a conversation to continue, encourage your child to keep sharing his thoughts and feelings without distracting from the communication through using occasional encouragers. These are brief indicators sprinkled throughout the conversation that let your child know you're interested and are following the conversation, encouraging him to continue. Some examples are: "Tell me more," "Yes," "Really?" "For instance?" "Uh-huh," and, "I see," while nodding your head.

Listen, really listen, using ECHO conversation skills. Be sure to repeat back to your child what you heard him saying, especially the feelings he seemed to be experiencing. Be careful to do this only after he has stopped talking to avoid interrupting.

Use open-ended questions. These questions are designed to draw out the person to whom you're talking. They should be used sparingly and will often help your child sort out his thoughts and feelings more thoroughly. Many parents, without even realizing it, tend to use closed-ended questions that serve to cut a conversation short and often come across as if you know how your child feels or what he should do. Closed-ended questions usually require only a one- or two-word answer. In comparison, open-ended questions request further elaboration. Here are some examples of both open- and closed-ended questions:

Avoid these	Instead say
"Did that make you angry?"	"How did that make you feel?"
"Was it a horrible experience?"	"What was it like for you?"
"How was school today?"	"What did you like most about school today?"

Focus on the relationship. During a conversation, it's important to remember the goal is to increase intimacy with your child. It's the conversation—the act of talking and sharing thoughts and feelings—that causes the increased sense of connection between the two of you. However, we often get distracted by the topic, and even more often by the solution. The most important part of a sharing time is *not* the solution but the feeling of intimacy. Although your child may be working toward a solution, it's more important that he be allowed to share for as long as necessary. Once a solution is presented, the conversation tends to be over. So remember, if your goal is to feel closer to your children, hold off on the solution until the sharing is complete.

"Shut Them Up"	*"Keep Them Talking"*
Changing the subject	Door-openers and invitations to talk
Closed by posture	Open, attentive body posture
Poor eye contact	Good eye contact
No or vague response	Occasional encouragers
Interrupting or holding the floor	Active listening
Closed-ended questions	Open-ended questions
Focusing on the solution	Focusing on the relationship and connection

Parenting in Practice

Fish-Bowl Conversations

OK, it's time again to apply what you've learned in a way that actually benefits your relationship with your children.

Getting the family talking to each other may not be as easy as it seems. I've realized over the years of trying to get families talking that the most difficult part is getting them started. They'd all just sit around looking at each other, waiting for someone to come up with a topic to discuss. To combat this awkwardness, I developed a list of "100 Conversation Starters" to help you out.

One of the best ways to use this list is to cut the topics apart and put them in a fish bowl. When you have set aside time to talk or just happen to have a little extra time, someone draws a topic out of the fish bowl and the discussion begins. Each person addresses the topic before drawing out the next one.

The assignment is a fun way not only to get conversations going, but also to learn things about each other you may never have known before. The more you know about each other, the more intimate the family relationships become. Feel free to add topics of your own. This assignment also can be a great car-trip or family-night activity.

100 Conversation Starters

1. If money were no issue, where would you like to travel?
2. If the house caught on fire and all your family were safe and you had time, what five things would you save?
3. If you inherited $100,000, what would you do with it?
4. What is your biggest regret?
5. What was your most embarrassing moment?
6. Describe a perfect evening.

7. Tell me about a special childhood memory.
8. What was your favorite Christmas and why?
9. Share a sad memory with me.
10. What things are you looking forward to this week, month, and year?
11. What do you like most about school or your job?
12. Tell me about your talents.
13. Tell me about something you fear.
14. If you could change one thing about yourself what would it be? Why?
15. What do you like best about yourself?
16. What's one of your favorite family memories?
17. If you could be any animal, what would you be? Why?
18. How would you like to see household responsibilities divided?
19. What do you think heaven will be like?
20. Tell me about your salvation experience.
21. Tell me about a spiritual high point in your life.
22. Tell me about a spiritual low point in your life.
23. What's the best advice you ever received?
24. If you could have three wishes, what would they be?
25. How can I show you that I love you?
26. Tell me about a time when God answered a prayer.
27. What makes you laugh?
28. Tell me your favorite joke.
29. What was or has been your favorite grade in school? Why?
30. Would you rather vacation in the mountains, at the ocean, or in a big city? Why?
31. What is your favorite fairy tale?
32. What kind of movies do you enjoy?
33. Would you rather be smart, beautiful, or famous? Explain.
34. When was the last time you cried?

35. If there had never been original sin, what do you think the world would be like?
36. If you could have picked anyone in the world to be your parents, who would you have picked?
37. Where would you like to live?
38. How could our family improve on how we settle arguments?
39. What would you consider to be your top five priorities in life?
40. What do you think my top five priorities are?
41. What are you feeling right now?
42. What are you thinking about right now?
43. What strengths do you see in me?
44. What would we do if our TV were out of order for one week?
45. Do you see me as a better giver or receiver? Explain.
46. What is your favorite recreational activity?
47. What is something we have never done together that you would like us to try?
48. What size box does the "perfect gift" come in? What would be inside?
49. List five of your "favorites" (food, color, game, movie, anything).
50. Describe your dream house.
51. If you could be anyone who ever lived for one day, who would you choose?
52. What's your most memorable experience?
53. Would you rather travel by car, plane, boat, or train?
54. What question would you like to ask God once you're in heaven?
55. What one experience would you like to have before you die?
56. What's the craziest thing you have ever done in public?
57. If you could choose any career, what would you be?

58. If you could spend a day with anyone who ever lived, who would you choose? Why?
59. Who would you like to visit once you're in heaven?
60. What "impossible" experience would you like to have?
61. What's a recreational activity you've never tried but would like to?
62. Tell me two things you "want" and two things you "need."
63. If you could have lived in any time period, which would you have picked?
64. Who has been the biggest positive influence in your life? Explain.
65. Tell me about your best friend.
66. What was the happiest time of your life?
67. If you were a writer, what would you write?
68. If you could trade lives with someone for a week, who would you trade with and why?
69. What is your favorite movie and why?
70. What do you worry about?
71. Name three things I used to do for you that you enjoyed that I have not done for a while.
72. What would be the first thing you'd buy if you won the lottery?
73. Where do you see yourself in five, ten, twenty years?
74. Describe the perfect Saturday.
75. Describe a favorite family tradition.
76. What kind of books do you like to read?
77. If you could ask God for a new talent, what would you ask for?
78. Are you a better spender or saver?
79. Would you rather have more time or more money?
80. What kind of music do you enjoy the most?
81. What do you want to be when you grow up?
82. What season of the year do you enjoy the most?

83. What holiday is your favorite?

84. Would you rather be hot or cold? Why?

85. If you had to lose one of your senses (touch, taste, smell, sight, hearing) which would you choose? Why?

86. Would you rather be deaf or blind? Why?

87. Is it easier to ask for forgiveness or to give it?

88. Tell me about a time you told someone about Jesus.

89. Who or what do you pray for?

90. What is something I can pray about for you this week?

91. What is your favorite Bible story? Why?

92. What is your least favorite Bible story? Why?

93. Do you like to be alone, with a few people, or in a crowd the most?

94. Would you prefer a dinner of home cooking, fast food, or gourmet restaurant fare?

95. Would you rather go to an art gallery, historical museum, or science center?

96. Would you rather go to an amusement park or the beach?

97. Who do you think has the hardest job in the world?

98. Who do you think has the easiest job in the world?

99. Tell everyone playing this game with you one thing you like about them.

100. Name three things you believe God has blessed this family with.

CHAPTER 10

BUT YOU ASKED ME IF I WANTED TO AND I DON'T

Parenting Isn't Polite

ॐ

"WOULD YOU PLEASE ...?"

When you're at a dinner party and you want the salt and pepper, all you have to do is ask, "Would you pass the salt and pepper, please?" The immediate response is almost always gracious, and you get what you wanted. That's how adults handle many things. We are working to be social and polite and still get done what we need to. We hear these polite requests all the time:

"Would you file this for me, please?"

"Can you stay a little late and finish that report?"

"Would you please show me your driver's license and insurance card?"

"Can I see you in my office?"

"Would you please be quiet during the movie?"

"Would you mind stepping into another line?"

As adults, we hardly even hear these as requests—and when they come from an authority figure, we immediately understand what the appropriate response to the request should be and give it without question if we care about the consequences.

Read back through the above questions and imagine answering each with a polite, "No thank you; I'd really rather not." What might happen? Some would obviously hold stronger consequences than others, but all would be met with shock and disbelief and a much-less polite response in return.

CHILDREN HAVEN'T DEVELOPED THE SOCIAL SKILLS TO UNDERSTAND WHEN A REQUEST MAY NOT REALLY BE A REQUEST AT ALL.

In parenting, we must remember we're not usually dealing with adults. This sort of question can become very confusing to a concrete and literal little brain. Children haven't developed the social skills to understand when a request may not really be a request at all. If you "ask" little Emily to please clean up her room, you'd better be prepared for either a yes or no response (and we can probably guess which it will be).

Children are doing their best trying to learn and understand language and communication, and that's hard enough by itself. Then add a bunch of adults who, from a child's perspective, don't even know the difference between a question and a command, and you have the perfect formula for confusion and chaos.

One of the first things you need to evaluate when you're struggling with apparently defiant behavior in your child is how you presented the task to the child. Did you ask your child to do something that's now not getting done? Well maybe the problem is you asked. As parents, we often try too hard to be polite to our kids. Although this may be proper etiquette in adult circles, it can be confusing to children.

To clarify, as you raise your children, you'll likely spend a significant amount of time teaching them to make choices by asking questions like "What would you like for lunch?" "Would you like to play outside today?" and "Will you be home in time for dinner?" Through these questions, your children are learning they have some control and choice in their world.

But what happens when you ask a question you really don't intend to have more than one answer, such as "Would you please set the table?" "Could you take out the trash before dinner?" or "Would you pick up your room, please?" Your child still hears these questions as just that—a question. To them, questions mean "I have a choice." So what are you going to do when Taylor says no?

If you are like most parents who haven't figured out their children don't understand the social graces of politely telling someone to do something, you might become angry and see your child as willfully disobedient. But in reality, they're not. You did ask. And when you send your child to her room for disobeying, you'll be sending one very confused child to isolation.

FROM A CHILD'S PERSPECTIVE

Some of the funniest experiences interacting with children are hearing some of their explanations of things they've heard, seen, or done. It really is true that kids say the silliest things, because they misunderstand the adult world and words around them. Consider these examples:

A dad was listening to his child say his prayer, "Dear Harold." At this, Dad interrupts and says, "Wait a minute. How come you called God 'Harold'?" The little boy looks up and says, "That's what they call him in church. You know the prayer we say, 'Our Father, who art in Heaven, Harold be thy name.'"

While watching his big brother's soccer game, a little boy asks his mother if he can have two dollars. She asks him why he needs it, and he says, "To go to the confessions stand, of course."

A big sister is trying to help her little brother understand why drinking orange juice will help him feel better and get over his cold. She tells him, "OJ is good for you because it has lots of Spider-Man C in it."

Mom recently bought a cell phone and has been having trouble remembering to take it with her when she leaves home. One day, her helpful little preschooler asks, "Mom, did you bring the celery phone?"

A young child walks up to Dad and asks, "What does neutered mean?" Dad looks around for help on this one, but finding none rummages through his brain for something to say. Before he gets a chance to answer, the child explains, "Mom says since Ben is having trouble with math, he has to be neutered."

> ℰℭ
>
> ────────────
>
> **IT'S OUR**
>
> **RESPONSIBILITY TO**
>
> **MAKE SURE OUR**
>
> **COMMUNICATION IS**
>
> **CLEAR AND**
>
> **UNDERSTANDABLE.**

And finally, here's one from our family.

When Taffeta was about three, she was being cared for by a good family friend named Sonya, who watched a couple of kids from church during the day. There was always lots of laughter in that home, and it never surprised me to have Sonya fill me in on the humorous things that had happened while I was away. One day, Sonya soberly said that she had to tell me about Taffeta and Blake (a little boy around the same age) getting in trouble that day for hitting each other over a toy.

This sounded like a serious offense to me, but Sonya started to crack up. She said she'd heard them yelling, and when she went to check, they were playing tug-o-war with a See-and-Say. As she walked into the room, the hitting and kicking started, but neither let go of the toy. I'm struggling to see the humor in this, but Sonya's laughter assured me it was coming.

Once the kids were separated and done with a time-out, Sonya tried to teach them about apologizing and making up. She had them face each other and told them, "Now, say you're sorry and shake hands." And that's exactly what they did. These two repentant three-year-olds looked seriously at each other, said "I'm sorry," and shook both of their own hands up and down in front of their bodies. Sonya was rolling, and now I was, too. The kids had done the best they could with a literal and concrete understanding of the concept "shake hands." And we got another good lesson to help us remember that kids really aren't miniature adults.

> **COMMANDS SHOULD BE SIMPLE, CLEAR, AND DIRECT.**

If kids have a hard time understanding the adult world's vocabulary, how much more confusing it must be to try to figure out whether or not a question is really a question. As parents, it's our responsibility to make sure our communication is clear and understandable—not only saying what we mean and meaning what we say, but doing so in a way our children really understand. Clear communication means that we understand our children's development level and then communicate at that level. But many of us talk to our kids just as we would any adult, and then we wonder why they don't seem to get what we mean.

To children, if a sentence ends with a question mark, they have more than one option for a correct response. If you intend only one correct response, don't ask. To communicate effectively with your child, take time to evaluate how you are using questions and commands.

Say your child is three. The question, "Would you like to go with me to the store?" gives the child the option of going or not going. But what if there's no one else home? Now "Would you like to go with me to the store?" seems a bit ridiculous. What if she says no? In this case, a question isn't the appropriate way to get your child ready to go to the store with you (since she doesn't really have a choice). Instead, this is a time for a command such as, "Please put on your shoes so we can go to the store."

Commands should be simple, clear, and direct. They don't leave room for questions or choice. The child knows what is expected of her when she hears a command clearly stated. Now if the child decides to ignore your command or say no, you simply remind her that this isn't a choice.

MIXED MESSAGES

Until you understand how your child hears questions vs. commands, you'll continue to be frustrated with what you think is direct defiance, and your child may be getting disciplined in very inconsistent (at least from her perspective) ways.

I've seen many parents who are confusing in their communication, then bring their kids in for treatment for poor behavior. As we evaluate what the parent has been trying, it quickly becomes evident it's the parent, not the child, who needs to make changes. Parents often phrase commands as questions to soften the blow, as if saying "would you please" will make their child smile about taking out the trash. It's not. And if the child hears it as a question, the trash may never get taken out at all. On the other hand, the same parents often state things in the form of a command that they never really intended to be a command at all.

For example, Julie's mom tells her to go put on her red dress. Julie goes to her room and sees her purple dress (her favorite) and puts it on instead. When she comes out, her mom is so glad that Julie got dressed on her own she doesn't say anything about the red dress.

Julie just received another confusing message. She heard a *command* to do something very specific and decided to do something different. Then, when her mother saw the command hadn't been obeyed, she did nothing. That sends the message that commands are really nothing more than suggestions, and that impression will come back to haunt Julie and her mom over and over in the future if not remedied.

When children receive mixed messages, parents get mixed responses. If they're asked a question and then get in trouble for not doing what they were supposed to do, they'll be confused. If they're given a command to do something and then not required to do it, they'll also be confused. If you want your children to do what you expect them to do, first clean up the issue of commands vs. questions.

USE COMMANDS ONLY WHEN YOU KNOW YOU HAVE THE TIME, ENERGY, AND MOTIVATION TO FOLLOW THROUGH.

COMMAND OR REQUEST—THAT IS THE QUESTION

We all want our children to experience and exercise a healthy sense of power in their world, and one of the most effective ways to give a child power is to give her choices. But the challenge for parents is to learn when a child should be allowed a choice and when she shouldn't. Reaching a healthy balance between giving choices and giving commands is difficult, but will ultimately be worth the work. Your child will learn to be independent by being given age-appropriate choices and taking responsibility for the outcomes of those choices. Also, your child will learn to respect and comply with authority by being presented consistently with commands that are enforced.

To decide when it's appropriate to give your child a choice or a command, start by evaluating the situation. Obviously, a situation in which someone's safety is at risk is *not* the time for a choice. "Would you please stop hitting your brother?" should never come out of any parent's mouth. You'll also definitely want to use a command when addressing established household rules and responsibilities. Curfew, bedtime, chores, and homework are command topics, not choices. It doesn't help to add "please" to the end of the command. Commands don't need to be polite.

If you're going to make an issue a command, make sure you plan to follow through and see the direction has been followed exactly as you commanded. Parents should use commands sparingly and only in situations where they intend to see to it the command is obeyed.

Telling a child to go put on her red dress is a command. If you just want her to get dressed and don't really care what she wears, make this a choice situation where she can exert some control and choose what she wears within guidelines. But if you're headed out for family pictures and specifically intend her to wear her red dress, a command is appropriate.

Once a command is given, it's your job to follow through and determine if compliance occurred. If you say, "Be home by ten o'clock," but your child is safe from consequences until ten fifteen, the command should have been, "Be home by ten fifteen." Saying what we mean and meaning what we say is extremely important when commanding. Your children know you better than you may think, and they learn quickly if you follow through on your commands or not. Use commands only when you know you have the time, energy, and motivation to follow through with what you've said. Otherwise, make it a choice within acceptable guidelines.

GIVING EFFECTIVE COMMANDS

Parents the world over tell or ask their children to change their behaviors at an amazingly high rate. One study shows young children are asked to change their behaviors once every six to eight minutes.[14] Can you imagine what it would feel like to be told you were doing something wrong or needed to do something different every six to eight minutes? I'm guessing this constant barrage of communication has something to do with how effective (or ineffective) our words are. Do we repeat the same command over and over because we don't see compliance? Do we make requests that are rejected so we have to retreat and try again with a command? We need to become more effective communicators if we don't want our kids to be "parent deaf" by the time they're twelve.

You can cut down on the number of commands and behavior-changing requests you give to your children by making the most of the commands you do give. Dr. Marilyn Heins, author of *ParenTips*, describes some common ineffective commands, then describes the necessary components of what she calls the "Effective Command."[15] The following information is based on her work.

A command could be ineffective in several ways. You may not be clear about who or what you're commanding, such as yelling, "Stop that!" in a room with several children. Commands are also ineffective if they're accompanied by a vague threat, such as "Finish your dinner or you'll be sorry." Children don't know what "you'll be sorry" really means. Also, commands are ineffective when paired with an unrealistic threat everyone in the room knows won't really happen, such as "If you don't get dressed, I'll take you to school naked." Finally, commands can quickly become ineffective if they sound more like begging or pleading: "Would you *please* just get along with your brother for a little while?"

We've identified how not to give a command; let's figure out the right way to do it. Here are Dr. Heins' tips for giving an "Effective Command":

Be close to the child. Trying to command a child from the other end of the house or even the next room won't be effective. If you can't make eye contact or lightly touch her on the shoulder, you're too far away.

Start with the child's name. This identifies exactly who you're talking to—and whom you expect compliance from. In our home, I'll say something I intend for one child, such as "Pick up your backpack," only to hear one or two others say, "I already did." I end up having to clarify to whom I was speaking, so why not just be clear from the outset?

Make a clear, concise statement. Avoid the types of aforementioned commands that can be difficult for children to understand. If they don't know exactly what you want, they can't comply. Also, present your command using the fewest words possible. Parents often fall into the trap of overexplaining, which teeters on lecturing.

Have a commanding expression on your face. Make your nonverbal communication serious and firm. You don't want to appear either angry or joking if you want your command to be effective.

Use a commanding tone of voice, but keep the volume down. Raising your voice or yelling isn't necessary for a command to be effective. As a matter of fact, they can make it less effective because children often tune out this type of communication. Speak in a soft yet firm tone to get their attention.

Omit the word "please." Just as you wouldn't expect an army sergeant to say "Attention! Please," you don't need to say please when commanding your children. Remember, you're not making a request, so you don't need to be polite.

Omit any words of warning. When you've determined the issue you're addressing is a command issue, understand this isn't the time to count to three or say, "Next time you do that...." You expect compliance immediately.

Don't give the child a choice. If you wanted your child to have a choice, you should have made a request, not a command.

Parenting in Practice

Family Game Night

One thing we've enjoyed most as a family is our family game night. We started it several years ago, and over time, our whole family seems to have become addicted to it. We try to choose at least one night a week (sometimes more) when we focus on playing all sorts of different games with our three children. These have been some of our most fun times together and are almost always filled with laughter. We take turns picking the games and make sure everyone can be involved in one way or another. Sometimes our youngest will be someone's helper on the games that are too difficult for him, but no one is ever left out. We've found if Mom and Dad forget that it's game night, one of the kids is always sure to remind us. We hope that even as they grow, they'll continue to want to keep one night a week open for game night.

CHAPTER 11

THE BIG NO-NOS OF PARENTING

Four Things to Avoid at All Cost

Remember our reality game-show contestants from the opening chapter of this book? Let's check back in with them for a moment right now....

Matt and Laura had grown to love their jungle over the past few years. The going got tough sometimes—really tough, as a matter of fact—but so far, those times had been fairly short-lived. Generally, they were enjoying this parenting game. They had won a few challenges with the help of the treasure map they received early on and were looking forward to continuing to explore their jungle as a family. It was about that time everything started to change again.

Early one morning, while Matt and Laura and the children were still sleeping, the reality-game host showed up unexpectedly, startling everyone out of dreamland. He announced in his loud voice it was time to move camp. Matt and Laura were stunned; they'd just gotten comfortable where they were. They finally knew their way around this part of the jungle and were doing pretty well meeting the needs of each member of the family. Why did they have to move? They pleaded briefly with the host to no avail. Everyone on the game knew the environment was always changing. That was part of the challenge.

They were allowed to grab one thing from their current camp before moving. With little hesitation, everyone quickly agreed to take the little treasure chest that held the map to their jungle. It had proved very helpful in the first phase of the jungle, and they knew they'd continue to need the information it provided on the upcoming challenges. So, with their little gold trinket in hand, they were off to another adventure.

As soon as they arrived at their new campsite, Matt and Laura quickly saw this part of the jungle was much rougher than from where they'd come. "Baby Jungle" had quiet, clear pools of water, level terrain, and lots of shade trees. But this place was altogether different. Danger lurked around every corner. The terrain was steep and dangerous, the waters were rough, and the shade was sparse at best.

The children quickly began exploring their new environment, sending Laura into immediate panic. She was grabbing hands and yelling, "Watch out!" "Don't go over there!" or "Stop doing that!" almost constantly. What happened to their nice, peaceful jungle? How would they ever manage this place?

They hadn't even had time to rest when the host appeared again to announce it was time for the next challenge to begin. What challenge? Surveying their new environment, Matt and Laura thought they had plenty of challenges ahead of them just to survive this part of the jungle. But they were about to get a new challenge whether they wanted it or not. That's how the game is played.

The new challenge included two major tasks. First, the parents needed to erect boundaries to keep their children safe in their new world. They were told there would be no way to protect the children from all the dangers in this part of the jungle, so they had to survey the environment, determine which dangers posed the highest threats to their children, and establish boundary markers around those areas.

Part two of the challenge would be even more difficult: explaining these boundaries to the children and getting them to respect and comply with them. Matt and Laura were warned that the explaining part might not be all that difficult, but the compliance part would make up for it. It would require extra energy from the parents to monitor their children's activities and determine if the boundaries were being respected. It was recommended to Matt and Laura that many parents in the past developed some sort of "insurance" to help assure their children respected the boundaries and their team could win this challenge. They received no further details or suggestions about the insurance, but they had a few ideas from watching previous game participants and were ready to meet this challenge head-on.

The parenting team soon decided which hazards they most wanted to protect their children from, with only a couple of differences. Using skills learned from their first little treasure box, they worked through these differences and agreed on a solution. They quickly erected the boundary markers and moved into part two much quicker than either had expected.

They took time to explain to their children the dangers of their new environment and the need for boundaries to protect them. Matt spelled out where the boundaries were and how the children were expected to stay within the limits set for them. Laura followed by informing the children if they did cross the boundaries, they'd experience consequences for doing so—but she didn't tell them what consequences they could expect, because she and Matt hadn't had time to develop them yet.

The couple had been so busy trying to complete the challenge in record time they hadn't stopped to decide what insurance they wanted to put in place. When they did have a couple of minutes to discuss it, they both felt assured insurance wasn't that important; their children would comply with the limits set because they were good kids. They were sure if it became a problem in the future, they could come up with something at that time.

Overall, that sounded like a fairly good plan. Matt and Laura's children had been well behaved and compliant up to now—but there was one little twist of which the parents were unaware.

To BE AN EFFECTIVE PARENT, YOU'LL NEED TO HONESTLY EVALUATE YOUR CURRENT STRATEGIES.

While they were busy erecting boundary markers, the host had a secret meeting with the children. He told the kids they also had a job during this challenge; it was up to them to test the parents. They were to check out all the boundary markers their parents established (some several times) to find out if the boundaries were strong enough to hold them back. If any boundary wasn't sturdy and strong, they were given permission to continue to cross it until their parents enforced it and made it secure. This would make it even harder for their team to win, but winning would create a safer environment overall.

So, unknown to the parents, their ordinarily easy-to-manage children had just become quality-control analysts, and they were entering the final phase of the challenge without insurance. Over the next few months, the children tested and retested the boundaries and found many of them unfortified and weak. As they crossed the boundaries over and over, they met frustrated and upset parents who had nothing of substance to remedy the situation.

The parents did try; the tools they were using just weren't

effective. They even seemed to rely on some of the same big, ineffective no-nos they'd watched other participants use. Before being drafted into the game, Matt and Laura had laughed at these tactics and assured themselves they'd never use them. "They simply don't work." But now, in their desperation, they were grasping at straws to get the kids to respect the boundaries.

The more Laura nagged and used idle threats, the more the kids disobeyed. Although Matt did better with coming up with actual consequences rather than just yelling, he, too, was failing to gain compliance from the children. The constant battle was wearing him out, and he'd often find himself enforcing the boundaries only when he felt up to it, or setting an appropriate consequence, then being too busy or exhausted to follow through. Other times, he'd just ignore the fact that the kids crossed the boundary again. He knew this inconsistency was confusing the children, but he didn't know what else to do.

Matt and Laura were exhausted and knew they were a long way from winning this challenge. If they hoped to turn the tide, they needed to realize they were using ineffective tools. They would have to stop relying on the big no-nos and replace them with tools that would really work.

KNOWING WHAT NOT TO DO

To be an effective parent, you'll need to honestly evaluate your current strategies and whether they're successfully teaching and training your children. Unfortunately, some strategies that many parents use are simply ineffective however you cut it. I call these "The Four Big No-Nos" of parenting.

These four mistakes almost always destroy and undermine a parent's proper authority. When an appropriate boundary is set and tested, responding in any one of these four ways will show the child the parent doesn't really mean what he or she says, which can be the beginning of the end of parental respect. If you're a normal parent, you've committed at least one of the following parental crimes. Don't beat yourself up; just take a minute to learn from your (and others') mistakes and start replacing these tactics with more effective skills.

LET'S SEE WHY THE FOUR BIG NO-NOS DON'T WORK

INCONSISTENCY

Jack and Ann have been struggling with a fairly new behavior from Carter, their four-year-old. He's learned that sticking his tongue out really seems to bother Mom and Dad—and that just seems to make him want to do it all the more. They've told Carter they expect this behavior to stop.

PARENT ENEMY NUMBER ONE IS MOST DEFINITELY INCONSISTENCY.

One evening at dinner, while Ann was finishing getting the food to the table, she heard Jack laughing. When she turned around, she saw Carter sticking his tongue out while making a funny face at his dad. As she watched, Carter did this several more times, and each time Jack laughed. When Ann finally said something, Jack remembered they'd been working with Carter to stop this behavior and immediately changed his response to a strong and stern, "Carter, stop that right now." Carter just laughed and did it again.

Steve was trying to finish some work he'd brought home from the office, but could hardly hear himself think over the roar of his daughter's stereo. He'd talked to Brenna several times about how loud she was allowed to play her music, and he was sure she was over the stated volume level. He waited as long as he could, hoping she'd decide on her own the music was too loud, but that didn't happen. When Steve entered Brenna's room and told her to turn the music down to the specified level, her response surprised him. She looked up at him and said, "Mom said I could play it this loud."

Shelly walked into her living room to find her two daughters jumping, rolling, cart-wheeling, and tumbling all over the furniture and floor. She stood there in shock; the girls knew the rule of no gymnastics in the house. The girls noticed her presence, but their behavior didn't change. Instead, they smiled and said, "Mom, watch what I can do." Once she got past her shock, she scolded the girls, "I can't believe what I'm seeing! You two know the rules. We *never* allow gymnastics in the house! Do you want to get in trouble?" Hearing Mom's tone, both girls stopped immediately, but looked surprised. "But Mom, you let us do it last week when Grandma and Papa were here."

Parent enemy number one is most definitely inconsistency. If we ever wanted to sabotage our ability to effectively parent our kids, all we'd have to do is be inconsistent. Disciplining for a particular offense one day then letting the same offense slide by another day only confuses a child. Also, if one parent says one thing and the other gives different instructions, the child is allowed to decide which parent he wants to obey today. It tells him to "go ahead and try it. It might be your lucky day."

Gambling's main attraction is the power of "maybe."

"Maybe this will be my lucky day."

"Maybe I'll win this time around."

"Maybe I'll prove them all wrong."

Maybes are a result of inconsistent outcomes. Sometimes I win, sometimes I lose—but at least sometimes I win. That's just enough to keep us trying.

Inconsistent parenting is much like that. Sometimes the child gets away with an offense and sometimes he doesn't. But he'll keep trying simply because he knows sometimes he can win.

If you want your children to learn once and for all that a particular offense will always be a loser, you have to show consistency about that offense.

LACK OF FOLLOW-UP AND FOLLOW-THROUGH

Today's parents are worn out, worn down, and worn thin. They're trying to move at the speed of light in five directions at once. We all know what it's like to try to manage home, work, school, church, outside activities, friends … the list goes on. We're understandably exhausted, distracted, and preoccupied.

NOT FOLLOWING THROUGH WITH WHAT WE SAY WILL PRODUCE KIDS WHO DON'T BELIEVE US AND, THEREFORE, WON'T OBEY US.

The result is we end up doing everything only halfway. We may start something but not really have time to finish it or do the job right before we're pulled off in another direction. We're constantly looking for shortcuts, time savers, and ways to reduce the amount of energy one activity takes to make room for the next. We're a microwave society that says if it can't be done in three minutes or less, it must not be worth doing.

Unfortunately, effective parenting and discipline don't work that way. Our children aren't little frozen dinners that can be ready to serve in minutes.

They take a lifetime to prepare, so we'd better just decide now they're worth it and we'll do our best to do it right. That means making sure we say what we mean and mean what we say ... and then follow through with it.

How often have you said, "If you ever do that again ..." or maybe, "This is your final warning; next time I see you doing that ..."? Maybe you meant it when you said it, but when the "next time" rolls around, you've completely forgotten about the warning or what the consequence was supposed to be.

Lack of follow-through also applies to positive reinforcers. I don't want to remember how many times Jim and I set up a star chart for our kids to help monitor and encourage certain behaviors. We'd take time to make the charts, talk to the kids about what was expected of them to earn a star, discuss the rewards they'd receive, and hang the charts where everyone could see.

These seemed to go well for a few weeks (usually because the kids were so excited about the rewards they'd make sure we reviewed the chart daily). But then we'd get busy and "forget" one day, and before we knew it we were trying to remember who did what for the past four or five days so we could catch up the chart. After this happened a few times, the chart would be forgotten entirely until someone (under four feet tall) would walk by and notice it and ask why they hadn't gotten any stars lately.

Whether it's a reward or a consequence, not following through with what we say will produce kids who don't believe us and, therefore, won't obey us.

The other side of this coin is the lack of follow-up. Sometimes we do remember the consequence we set for a particular behavior, and we do it. The problem isn't that we forgot what we said, but that we don't follow up what we said to completion.

If you ground your son from television for a week, do you

check up on day four to make sure he's not watching, or does he innocently sit down with the rest of the family to watch everyone's favorite show? Do you walk by your son's room, see him on the computer and not even remember he lost all computer privileges—or, even worse, just decide you don't have the energy to deal with it right now? Do you promise your child you'll take him out for ice cream if he makes his bed every day this week, then, when he does, put off the outing because something else came up?

These scenarios are common but dangerous.

IDLE THREATS

"If you don't get dressed right now, I'll take you to school naked!"

"I'm about to ground you for the rest of your life!"

"If you don't stop acting like that, the rest of us will go to the movie and leave you here alone" (this said to a child much too young to be left alone).

"You'll do what I said or you can go sit in your room for the next year."

It would be nice if parents didn't make threats at all, but we especially shouldn't make idle threats. Making a threat you have no real intention of following through on only undermines your ability to set effective consequences for misbehavior.

Idle threats like those above are usually made in haste and out of frustration and anger. Our emotions get out of control, and we start running off at the mouth. In the heat of the moment, we may mean what we say, and our children may even believe it briefly. But once things settle down, everyone involved usually realizes it's really not going to be that way.

Telling your four-year-old you'll leave him home while you go to church if he doesn't get his shoes on right now may scare him into hustling into those loafers, but what happens when your little one calls your bluff? You'll be back-peddling fast, trying to find a way to prove *you're* the one who's supposed to be calling the shots—but he probably won't believe you for long.

Idle threats send mixed messages that lead to confusion, doubt, and rebellion for the child. Idle threats actually train our kids to rebel against what we say. When they challenge a threat we give, they expect us to hold strong to our words and maintain that limit. But because we didn't really mean it when we said it or it was something we could never really do, we have to back down. The child hears, "It's OK not to do what I said, because I'm not really going to do what I said either." Your actions are louder than your words, and your behavior tells him you often don't mean what you say.

> **ONCE NAGGING BEGINS, IT BECOMES A NEVER-ENDING CYCLE THAT FEEDS ON ITSELF.**

NAGGING

Many parents find themselves sucked into the black hole of nagging. The more they nag, the further away from effective parenting they seem to get. Once nagging begins, it becomes a never-ending cycle that feeds on itself and requires more and more nagging to get the job done.

From what I can tell, nagging begins as a parent's good intention that somehow goes astray. A parent gives a command, but doesn't get a response right away. Instead of intervening right then, the parent decides to fire a warning shot in the form of a reminder. Either way, it's intended to give the child "one more chance" to be compliant.

I'm not saying that giving a reminder or warning of consequences is wrong. As a matter of fact, as a child is working on learning a new skill or responsibility, a single reminder or warning can effectively help the learning curve along. However, the problem comes when the single reminder turns into another and another and another ... and before you know it, you've been completely sucked into the Twilight Zone, where your child seems to have changed completely from the responsible and intelligent human being you used to know into an apparently unintelligent life form that can't seem to do anything on its own.

Once the reminder turns into nagging, the responsibility of completing the chore seems to move from the child to the parents—who, not wanting to do the chore themselves, continue to nag (eventually expending more energy than it probably would have taken to do it themselves). This wears out the parents, teaches the child to rely on others as his memory and motivation, and increases parent-child conflicts.

The other problem with nagging is it eventually seems to lead to selective hearing loss in your children. As the problem persists, children seem to become completely deaf to the first several reminders given by the parent because they know from experience the first ones don't really matter. In response, the parent increases the decibel level of the commands just to get through. Eventually, the volume, tone, or body language build to a point that grabs the child's attention, and the job gets done—leaving an exhausted and crippled parent in their wake.

The more parents nag, the more children expect it, and the better they get at knowing when they should listen if they don't want to suffer serious consequences. As parents, we give signals that tell the child when we really mean it, even if we aren't aware of doing it.

Now that I'm an adult, I can see how this specific no-no played out in my own home growing up. As a young teen, one of my chores was to unload and load the dishwasher. I didn't particularly enjoy it, but it was definitely better than some of the other chores available, so I didn't complain much. However, it didn't rank very high in my priority list and was very easy to ignore or "forget."

Now, my dad is a fairly large man and can seem threatening and intimidating at times, but usually he was just a big teddy bear. He'd work hard all day and come home in the evening hoping to just sit and relax in his chair. After dinner, Mom or my little sister would clean off the table, Dad would head for his chair, and I'd go to my bedroom to call my best friend I hadn't talked to in at least forty-five minutes. Then it would start.

"Debbie, you need to get in the kitchen and do the dishes," Dad would say, just loud enough for me to hear down the hall.

"OK, I'll be right there," was my polite reply. Then I'd tell my friend I needed to get off the phone in "just a little while." I knew my father's signals well enough to know I probably had about twenty minutes of talk time left.

Several minutes later, Dad would fire his first warning shot. "Debbie" (a little louder than before), "I told you that the dishes need to be done."

"On my way" was followed by, "I'm going to have to get off the phone soon," to my friend.

Dad would quickly get involved in the nightly news, and several more minutes (how long would depend on how interesting the news was that evening) would pass before a second and more serious warning shot.

"Debra Lynne! I'm not going to tell you again. Go get those dishes done!" The decibel level definitely had increased, and I knew my time was getting short—but wasn't up yet.

"Coming!" was the response he'd hear. "I've got about five more minutes" was what my friend heard.

In about five minutes, the final warning was given, but in my house, this wasn't a verbal signal. Because my dad is a hard worker and a fairly large man, he didn't want to have to get out of his chair once he was in it and comfortable—thus the yelling down the hall. But when the yelling seemed to be falling on deaf ears, one sound would always shake the house (or at least my little section of it)—the sound of my daddy's foot sliding off his other leg (from sitting cross-legged in his comfortable chair) and his boot hitting the floor.

START LOOKING FOR OPPORTUNITIES TO TELL YOUR CHILDREN WHAT THEY'RE DOING RIGHT.

Daddy was in motion! That *always* seemed to get through to my eardrums and catapulted me into motion. Faster than a speeding bullet, I would jump off my bed, hang up the phone, and run down the hall and through the living room just in time to see Dad raising himself off his chair. As he saw me fly through the room, he'd relax back into his chair saying, "It's about time." All would be at peace again.

Children of parents who nag become very good at knowing just when they "have to" respond. They know when the parent is just about at the end of their rope and have learned to respond just in the nick of time to avoid serious consequences. If you find yourself nagging, and your child does seem to respond eventually, watch and listen to yourself to learn what signals you're sending.

It's probably the last thing you said or did that finally got a rise out of your child. You need to learn to say or do that thing once, followed by no more than one "warning shot" (depending on the situation; older children and teens shouldn't even need the warning). If they don't respond, then they should be hit with a consequence immediately. This will keep the parent from getting frustrated and angry after repetitive "reminders" and help the child be more responsible.

PARENTING IN PRACTICE

CATCH 'EM BEING GOOD

So often we parents spend more time telling our kids what they're doing wrong or need to change than we do telling them something they've done just the way we hoped. A great parenting strategy is to catch 'em being good.

All you have to do is start looking for opportunities to tell your children what they're doing right. Often we walk through a room where our children are sitting quietly reading a book, playing their favorite electronic game, or simply coloring a picture, and we just keep walking. Why not take a second or two to tell your children that you appreciate how they're behaving?

Take time to thank them for getting ready on time, doing a chore without being asked, or smiling when you woke them up. Big or little, it doesn't really matter; they'll love hearing what you love about them. Set a goal to catch your kids being good a minimum of three times a day.

CHAPTER 12

THE POWER TOOLS OF PARENTING

Attention and Ignoring

$\mathbf{A}$ few years back, I learned the importance of having some real power tools around the house. It was late spring, and Jim and I had decided a great gift for the kids would be one of those all-wood, do-it-yourself swing or play sets. We shopped around until we found just the right design with all our favorite attachments. It absolutely had to have a slide, two swings, and a fort. Jim thought the fireman's pole was great, and we both wanted the extra two-person swing for ourselves. By the time we'd designed the perfect playground and loaded up all the necessary lumber, I was sure we'd bought enough to build a whole house (well, maybe just a little one).

Once we arrived home, the unloading process began— one piece at a time. It seemed to take *forever*. Before long, I was ready to offer those men at the lumberyard as much money as it took to get them to come and unload this stuff into the backyard just like they'd loaded it into the truck— effortlessly. Somehow, Jim convinced me that wasn't necessary and we could do this all by ourselves. So I pulled myself back up and grabbed one end of a four-by-four, determined to do my part. Before long, the truck was empty. Even though the pieces in the backyard looked like a life-size jigsaw puzzle, I was thankful all the *hard work* was done.

My plan was to go inside and put the kids down for a nap while Jim put together the new equipment. I expected the kids would be ready to go play on their new swing set after a couple hours of rest, and I expected the swing set would be ready—how very wrong I was.

When the naps were over and we ran outside to swing, we met a disappointing site. What was supposed to be fort, slide, swing, and other fun things looked nothing like that. It looked more like a pile of lumber that had just been moved around the yard. I was obviously frustrated, but I tried to ask Jim a question that wouldn't sound too emotional.

"What's the problem? I thought the kids would be able to play on this when they woke up." The look I received told me he not only thought I was absolutely nuts for thinking such a thing, but also that he never had any such expectation. "You've got to be kidding," was all he attempted to say, and he went back to work.

I really wanted to know why this was taking so long. The answer was something like, "Do you see what I'm trying to work with here? Cutting through a four-by-four with a hand saw tends to take a while. Here, why don't you try it?"

Being the stubborn, "anything you can do I can do better" type of girl, I grabbed the saw and said, "Where do I cut?" Jim showed me and stood back. I pushed and pulled that stupid saw with all my might, but it hardly moved. At one point, I put all my weight into it and actually made about two full strokes before the saw abruptly caught on something and stopped with no warning. I went flying backwards, to be caught by my laughing husband.

"OK, OK. So it's harder than it looks. How long do you think it will take?"

"Using these tools? Oh, about six months," was his sarcastic reply.

I didn't think he was serious, but about a week later I was beginning to think maybe he was. The lumber still looked more like a pile than a play set, and I was beginning to think the kids would be teenagers before they'd get to play on the thing. When Jim and I had time to sit down and talk about it, he told me that he just didn't have the tools he needed to do the job right. I wanted the job done and done right, so we went off in search of—you guessed it—the perfect power tools!

As we walked into the "boy toy" store, my husband's face lit up. I had no idea tools could be so exciting—especially the plug-in kind. Jim and the salesman were having a wonderful time discussing things like horsepower and watts, speed and blade sizes, and many other things that made no sense to me. But if this was what it took to get the job accomplished, I was all for it.

YOU NEED TO EVALUATE YOUR CHILDREN AND WHAT THEY NEED TO BECOME RESPONSIBLE ADULTS.

We left the store with several new gadgets and a new supply of expectations—but these expectations were about to come true. Jim "The Tool Man" was on the job, smiling from ear to ear each time he hooked up one of his new power tools. I soon saw the lumber begin to look more like the picture of the swing set we'd picked out a few weeks before. Having the right tools available made his job so much easier.

Don't get me wrong—the original tools would have gotten

the job done eventually (hopefully before the kids' wedding days). But the power tools not only helped accomplish the task much quicker, but allowed Jim to make better use of his energy—not to mention making him feel more effective and in control. You gotta love a man and his power tools!

What Do Power Tools Have to Do with Parenting?

When you have a major job to do, you want the most powerful and effective tools at your disposal. Regular tools can and will get the job done eventually, but they take a lot of physical effort and time. Or you can pull out the power tools (listen to the roar!) and get the job done much quicker and with much less effort.

The same principle is true in parenting. Parenting is definitely a major job, and many different tools are available to us. Some will take considerably more effort and energy, and it will take longer before their effect is noticed. We can use those tools or identify the "power tools" that take the least amount of effort and show the quickest result. The power tools of parenting allow the parent to feel the most effective and in control.

Determining the necessary tools requires evaluating the job. When Jim looked at the job, he knew what tools he needed. The wood required a saw and a drill to become a swing set. As a parent, you need to evaluate your children and what they need to become responsible adults.

What Are These Kids Looking For?

Katilyn, eighteen months old, sits in her high chair eating lunch. Dad sits beside her encouraging her to eat while he reads the newspaper. Katilyn accidentally drops her spoon, which receives a quick response from Dad. He gives her a soft rebuke as he hands her spoon back and goes back to reading his newspaper. She drops the spoon again, not accidentally this time, and the game begins.

Blake is ten and has just learned a new skateboard trick he can't wait to show his parents. When he gets home from his friend's house, Mom is there waiting for him. He excitedly begs her to come out and watch the trick. As she follows him out the door, he can hardly contain himself; he grabs his board and begins his show. He's thrilled when she sits down to watch and knows she's not in a hurry to get back inside. He repeats the trick over and over with cheers and applause from the front porch. Before he finishes, Dad drives up, and it starts all over again.

Tristan is in the middle of a "terrible-twos" temper tantrum. He just wanted to pet the goldfish. Why did Mom have to say that bad word: "No, no"? Then, when he tried again, she moved him off the stool and put him in the next room all by himself. This just can't be right—and the "I'm not getting my way" tantrum begins.

Amy is fifteen going on twenty-five and is sure she has the whole world figured out. She's so busy with sports, clubs, and social time she seems to hardly ever be at home or spend time with her family. Although she misses them from time to time, she's generally fine with how things are. Her parents are there to take her where she needs to go and to give her money when she needs it; other than that, they're busy doing their own thing, too.

Then Amy has a really bad day at school. When she gets home, she slams the door, throws down her books, and stomps into the kitchen to make herself a snack. Just then, Dad comes home and reminds her to unload the dishwasher. She yells, "Is that all I'm here for, just to be your slave? Can't a girl just get something to eat without having to be told what to do?" Without thinking Dad yells back, "Don't you talk to me that way young lady!" and the fight is on.

What do each of these children have in common? What are they so desperately seeking? What they need more than anything becomes evident as we examine their very first job ever.

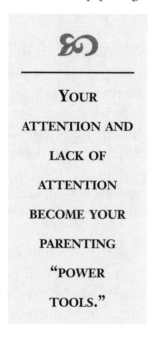

YOUR ATTENTION AND LACK OF ATTENTION BECOME YOUR PARENTING "POWER TOOLS."

YOUR VERY FIRST JOB

You may say your very first job was lawn-mowing, babysitting, or working at a fast-food restaurant. But your first job actually goes back much further than that—back to the day of your birth. Babies are born with one very basic instinctive need, one desire and one desire only, and that becomes their "job": to gather as much *attention* as possible.

Most babies are very good at it. What do we do at their very first cry and almost every cry thereafter? We pay attention. We check on them, give them what they need, cuddle them, and speak to them in funny voices. They soon learn crying isn't the only behavior that gets them attention. They realize that smiling, rolling over, crawling, and throwing the toy on the floor over and over also get those around them (mainly parents) to ooh and ahh over them.

As babies grow, their job remains the same—only the means of meeting the job requirements changes. Eventually, rolling over becomes routine, and the parents give it less and less attention. But before long, the child tries a new skill, and the gushing attention comes again—at least until the new skill becomes the norm.

As children experiment to find the most effective means of gaining the attention they need, they learn some behaviors gain strong positive attention and others seem to just be ignored. But eventually, they learn the attention available to them isn't all coos and cuddles. They learn what it's like to experience negative attention.

That first dose of negative attention often causes a quivering bottom lip and very leaky eyes, quickly followed by a heartbroken cry. The first slap on the hand or loud "No!" is met with shock and dismay. But the child has just learned where the emergency supply of attention is stored. When all else fails and attention levels are running low, she can head for the electrical outlet or Mom's favorite collectible and get a quick dose of attention, albeit negative.

Let's look at the four children described earlier and how they're getting their job done. Katilyn learns she can get her dad to look away from the newspaper and go from giving her no attention to giving her some attention (even if it's a little negative) by dropping her spoon. Blake searches for and receives positive attention from his mom. He can't seem to get enough of it and soaks up the applause and cheers.

YOUR CHILD'S JOB IS TO SOAK UP AS MUCH ATTENTION AS POSSIBLE.

Tristan receives a small dose of negative attention by being told, "No, no." But then, when he tries it again, he gets removed from the room, resulting in getting no attention at all and sparking the fit as a desperate attempt to gain any attention. Finally, Amy, obviously needing a strong dose of positive attention, puts herself in a position to receive a strong dose of negative attention.

Please note: Your children aren't openly attempting to manipulate you or others. They're not aware attention-getting is their "job"; it's just what they do naturally. But even though they're not consciously aware of this strong internal drive, they are motivated by this very basic need. Therefore, your attention and lack of attention become your parenting "power tools."

IF YOU WANT YOUR CHILD TO FEEL TREASURED, SUPPLY HER WITH AS MUCH POSITIVE ATTENTION AS YOU POSSIBLY CAN.

A Note of Clarification: Take a moment here to be sure you understand that in this chapter I'm addressing attention-seeking behaviors specifically. In contrast, some of a child's behaviors are more directly geared toward testing limits and exerting independence. How to best respond to those types of behaviors and to direct disobedience are the topics of other chapters. Don't assume the skills taught in this chapter (i.e., ignoring) would be sufficient or even appropriate when dealing with direct defiance. That said, let's turn our attention to dealing with attention-seeking behavior.

WHAT ARE MY CHOICES?

Giving or withholding your attention has the most impact on a child's basic attention-seeking behaviors, present and future. The behavior you give attention to in your child is being reinforced and, therefore, will be repeated, while the behavior you ignore isn't reinforced and, therefore, begins to decline. Your child's job is to soak up as much attention as possible. Children who are ignored for extended amounts of time will begin looking for ways—positive or negative—to get attention.

Let's look at the three choices parents have in responding to any of your child's attention-seeking behavior:

THE PARENT CAN GIVE POSITIVE ATTENTION

> What is man that you make so much of him, that
> you give him so much attention ...? (Job 7:17)

God attends to us in many positive ways. We know he blesses us, protects us, forgives us, and loves us unconditionally. Why does he pay so much attention to us? After all, he's almighty, all powerful, King above all kings, etc. With all that he is and all that he has, why does he even notice us? Because he loves us, and we are so very important to him.

We tend to give our attention to people and things that are important to us. We should value our children just as our Heavenly Father values us. Therefore, we should want to give them our attention. If you want your child to feel treasured, supply her with as much positive attention as you possible can.

Positive attention is anything you add into your child's environment that she considers pleasant and makes her feel good—such as praise and compliments, encouragement, hugs and kisses, pats on the back, smiles, and more.

Remember: Your child can never get enough of this type of attention. She'll always have room for more—so pour it on!

THE PARENT CAN GIVE NEGATIVE ATTENTION

> O LORD, do not rebuke me in your anger or discipline
> me in your wrath. (Ps. 6:1)

Not all attention is positive. There are all kinds of negative attention, and unfortunately, this seems to be all many children receive. There's a time and place for some forms of negative attention, such as appropriate discipline and rebuke, but some other forms should have no place in our lives, especially not with our children (i.e., name-calling, physical and emotional abuse).

God, our model parent, uses negative attention sparingly and with control. He does discipline those he loves and expects us to do the same. However, negative attention isn't his primary means of interacting with us. His main focus isn't giving us pain and suffering, but rather supplying us with grace and mercy. What a wonderful model to follow!

> **ALTHOUGH APPROPRIATE REBUKE AND DISCIPLINE ARE NECESSARY AT TIMES, THEY SHOULD COME OUT OF YOUR LOVE.**

Negative attention is anything unpleasant you add into your child's environment. Even if these things are placed there for your child's own good, such as physical discipline, they're considered negative because they're unpleasant from the child's point of view. Negative attention includes critical or derogatory comments, negative touch (such as spanking and thumping on the head), making fun of them, yelling, etc.

Remember: Although appropriate rebuke and discipline are necessary at times, they should come out of your love for your child rather than your anger. These interactions should never be either physically or emotionally abusive. You should work hard to keep the negative attention in your home to a bare minimum, only used when absolutely necessary. It should never be your primary means of interacting with your child.

THE PARENT CAN COMPLETELY IGNORE THE CHILD'S BEHAVIOR

> Indeed, God does not listen to their empty plea; the Almighty pays no attention to it. (Job 35:13)

One final way God interacts with his children is by withdrawing his attention from them. We know that when there's unconfessed sin in our lives, our fellowship with God is broken and he doesn't hear our prayers. This is the ultimate "ignoring." God ignores his children to show his disapproval of their wrong behavior and as a way to extinguish it. Parents also should learn to effectively use withdrawing of attention from our children to decrease their inappropriate actions.

Remember: Ignoring involves the *total* withdrawal of attention—absolutely no verbal comments, no looks, no touch, *nothing!*

PAY ATTENTION TO ME!

GATHERING NEGATIVE ATTENTION USUALLY HAPPENS WHEN CHILDREN FEEL POSITIVE ATTENTION ISN'T AVAILABLE.

Children don't know it, but they can get only three reactions to their attention-getting "job." They can receive your positive attention, your negative attention, or none of your attention through being ignored (which means to them they aren't doing their job).

Of these three possibilities, children always prefer positive attention. They never seem to get enough. They love it when you hug them (at least up to a certain age), when you brag on them, when you tell them how wonderful you think they are, and when you compliment and praise them. We never outgrow this desire to receive positive attention from those around us.

Now, let's say your job is to gather as much attention as possible and then you realize your first choice, positive attention, isn't available. Well, you go to the next best thing. As odd as this may sound, when you have only three choices available, the next best thing is negative attention—at least it's still attention. The third choice is no attention at all, and children won't choose it.

IGNORE ANY NEGATIVE OR INAPPROPRIATE BEHAVIOR YOU POSSIBLY CAN.

So, gathering negative attention usually happens when children feel positive attention isn't available—at least, not at a sufficient level to satisfy and fill them. They can go for short periods of time (how long depends on the child) with no attention at all when they've been satisfied by a good supply of positive attention. However, once the reserve starts to deplete, they'll head out to find more attention. They'll look for positive attention as long as possible, but when the reserve reaches a critically low level, they head for that emergency supply called negative attention.

I'm sure many of you have experienced this in your own homes. How many times have you felt like your child was arguing just for the sake of arguing? Or said something like, "Why do you do that? You know it's just going to get you in trouble? How many times do I have to tell you to stop doing that"?

These may be indications your child is running low on positive attention and is now in search of that emergency supply of negative attention. It's not premium quality attention, but it still fills up the tank and gets her going again. Remember that any attention-seeking behavior that gains negative attention from you goes into the emergency-supply fund to be tapped in the future if needed. So as you learn to use this first power tool of parenting, the most important instruction is this:

- Whatever behavior you give your attention to (either positively or negatively) will be reinforced.

Attending to your child's positive behaviors with compliments and statements of appreciation will help her want to continue that behavior. However, attending to your child's negative-attention-seeking behavior also will reinforce it and make it more likely to reoccur. Because of its reinforcing nature, negative attention should be used sparingly, only for direct acts of disobedience or when other forms of discipline have proved ineffective.

Now let's consider your other power tool: withholding your attention.

THE POWER OF IGNORING

Ignoring is very powerful to a child because it means she's not doing her job at all; she's not gathering any attention. Children will do just about anything to avoid being ignored. As a matter of fact, when given the choice between negative attention and being ignored, the child will choose negative attention every time.

Once again, I'm not saying this is a conscious choice. If you ask a child directly, "Would you rather have a spanking or go to your room for thirty minutes?" most would consciously choose the room to avoid the pain of the spanking. But on the whole, if the ignoring goes on too long, she'll actually start seeking out negative attention. She'd rather be yelled at than ignored.

That's why it's a parenting power tool. When a child will do practically *anything* to avoid something, just think of the *anythings* you as a parent could think of to get her to do and how you could use this tool to shape a more responsible future adult.

The main instruction for using the power tool of ignoring is this:

* Attention-seeking behaviors that are completely ignored will begin to disappear.

IGNORING IS MOST EFFECTIVE WHEN PAIRED WITH THE OTHER POWER TOOL OF POSITIVE ATTENTION.

Start by identifying behaviors you don't like in your child. Actions you've been giving negative attention to in hopes of extinguishing are great first choices. Now that you understand the negative attention you've been handing out has actually done the exact opposite of what you hoped, it's time to start ignoring.

The rule of thumb is to ignore any negative or inappropriate behavior you possibly can. Of course, you're not going to choose to ignore your daughter as she takes a swing at her little sister or runs out into the street. Physical protection should overrule just about any parenting strategy. However, if the behavior is *not* going to cause significant damage to person or property and if it's *not* a direct act of disobedience or defiance, it probably can be ignored. We could choose to ignore many behaviors we don't like in our children instead of yelling at them, actually reinforcing their behavior through negative attention. For example, do you yell or ignore when your children seek unhealthy attention through misbehaviors such as the following:

- Jumping on the furniture
- Picking their noses
- Running down the hall
- Throwing a temper tantrum
- Getting up from the table during dinner
- Whining

These are just a few of the many behaviors that could be effectively ignored and therefore extinguished.

Ignoring is most effective when paired with the other power tool of positive attention. Let's say your child is misbehaving and you're effectively ignoring the behavior. Next, start looking for a chance to give positive attention for a different behavior, really focus on trying to "catch 'em being good." As soon as your child starts an appropriate behavior, stop your ignoring and replace it with positive attention for the new behavior. Since your child's job is to gather attention, you've just effectively shown her which behavior gets no attention and which gets positive attention. Believe me, she'll start remembering which is which.

Warning: As with any power tool, the principle of ignoring must be used with caution, and the instructions should be followed carefully to avoid harm to anyone involved—in this case, your child. The concept of ignoring is so powerful that if not used sparingly and appropriately, it can seriously damage the person being ignored. Parents who chronically ignore their children to the point of neglect will inflict long-term emotional damage on that child.

When working with adult survivors of physical abuse vs. survivors of parental neglect, those suffering from chronic neglect show much more significant damage and emotional scars. I've even heard adult survivors of chronic neglect say, "I wish he would have hit me. At least then I would have known he knew I was alive!" When a child regularly can't get the attention she needs and seeks out, the long-term effect of being ignored is that she begins to feel completely worthless, unimportant, and invisible. That's not how to use the power tool of ignoring.

WHEN TO ATTEND AND WHEN NOT TO

Now that you understand why to use these power tools, let's talk about how and when to use them.

In interacting with your children, you know you want them to keep doing some attention-seeking behaviors and stop doing others. However, if you're like many parents I've talked with, you may be doing things exactly backwards.

Let's say you've had an exhausting day at work and just arrived home. All you want is a few minutes of peace and quiet to relax and settle down, and you hope the kids are occupied with something that doesn't require your attention right now.

Well, it's your lucky day! Jordon is next door playing, and Katie is sitting quietly on the floor coloring a picture. You walk softly to your favorite chair, so as not to disturb the artist at work, and lie back to rest. You noticed Katie coloring and think, "Shhh. Don't say a word; she's being good. Don't mess with a good thing." You close your eyes and are about to drift off to sleep when a loud squeal startles you back to reality. Your quiet little artist is jumping up and down as hard as she can on the sofa and squealing at the top or her lungs. Without even thinking, you immediately yell, "Katie, get off the couch! You know better than that. How many times do I have to tell you, 'we don't jump on the furniture!' Now get down and be quiet!" She jumps off the couch with a huge thump that makes the pictures on the wall shake and stomps off to the next room.

This is a fairly normal encounter for many parents—and an example of doing things exactly backwards. You ignored the behavior you liked and hoped would continue (quiet coloring) and chose to pay attention to the behavior you disapproved of and wanted to stop (squealing and jumping). The fact that the attention you gave was negative means very little—it was still attention. Katie's only other choice right then was getting ignored.

Now let's look at how this encounter could have gone using the principles of attention and ignoring in your favor.

Coming home from an exhausting day at work, you notice Katie sitting quietly on the floor coloring. You know you need to relax for a few minutes and would love Katie to stay interested in what she's doing, so you give her some positive attention and praise her artistic endeavors. "Hi, Katie. Wow! I love that picture you're coloring. I can't wait to see it when it's finished." You lie back in your chair. She's sitting over there enjoying what she's doing and soaking in the positive attention you just gave her. In a few more minutes (how long depends on your individual child) you quietly notice her again. "Katie, thank you for coloring so quietly. I love what you're making." And the peace and quiet goes on. Katie might stay there for twenty to thirty minutes with just a few simple words of encouragement.

Now let's say you forgot to praise Katie for coloring quietly. It never even crossed your mind to apply positive attention until you hear the loud squeal and find her jumping up and down on the sofa. Is it too late to salvage your new parenting plan? Absolutely not!

If you were quietly ignoring Katie being good, then realize it when you find yourself wanting to yell at her; just take a deep breath and wait. She was sitting there coloring and soon realized she wasn't doing her job—she wasn't gathering any attention. So she started looking for a new behavior that would draw any attention at all, even negative. She remembers last week she was jumping on the couch and you yelled at her. That should work. So off she heads for the sofa. Remember *any* behavior that draws your attention *will* be repeated.

Now that you're faced with negative behavior, think, "Is this behavior endangering herself, others, or property?" Probably not. So the choice right now would be to ignore her jumping on the furniture. Simply pretend you don't see it. Hide behind your newspaper or close your eyes and wait for your next opportunity to catch her being good—it will come.

Katie is going to be confused right about now, because jumping on the furniture has always attracted your attention in the past. She'll soon realize she's still being ignored, which is very wrong, so she'll start to escalate and try something different. "I bet if I jump real hard off here and make a loud noise you'll pay attention to me." Off she goes, taking the biggest leap she can and hoping for the loudest bang. As soon as her feet hit the floor you pop up, look her in the eyes and say, "Katie, I love it when your feet are on the floor! Thank you. Can you show me how you can skip?" and things are back on track.

Don't forget, any behavior that you let go by unnoticed will probably soon drop away, but be sure not to ignore attempts and successes at making positive changes. If you do, your child will likely stop trying in those areas as well. Noticing and encouraging positive behaviors and attempts to change and ignoring negative traits and slip-ups is one of the most effective ways to parent your child. Give positive feedback and comment on what she's doing right. The power of praise is immeasurable.

Parenting in Practice

Through Your Child's Eyes

This exercise will help you evaluate yourself through the eyes of your child. Put yourself in your child's position and look from her perspective. How do you help your child meet her job requirements? When our children have homework or a school project, most of us get right in there to help however we can. Without doing it for them (hopefully), we provide whatever's needed for them to do their very best. Let's also do that for their biggest assignment ever: gathering attention.

Ask yourself the following questions and evaluate yourself as honestly as possible. Wherever you place yourself, there will most likely be room for improvement. Focus the next thirty days on changing how you use your power tools, then evaluate yourself again at the end of the thirty days.

1. I am actively participating in helping my child get his or her full quota of attention each day.

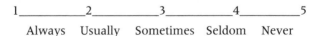

1_____2_____3_____4_____5
Always   Usually   Sometimes   Seldom   Never

2. The majority of attention I give my child is premium quality (positive attention) rather than emergency-supply quality (negative attention).

1_____2_____3_____4_____5
Always   Usually   Sometimes   Seldom   Never

3. If asked, my child would report I ignore her more than I give either positive or negative attention.

1_____2_____3_____4_____5
Always   Usually   Sometimes   Seldom   Never

CHAPTER 13

THE INS AND OUTS OF EFFECTIVE DISCIPLINE

Learning What Will Really Work

ॐ

May I have your attention please?

Get ready, because I, Debbie the Great, am about to attempt the impossible. Keep your eyes on the following pages, and you'll see one of the most impressive illusions of all time. In the next few pages, right before your very eyes, I'll attempt to reduce the volumes of books on discipline into one simple chapter. I know; you're amazed I'd consider such a feat—as am I. I'll use no camera tricks or other special effects. What you are reading is actually happening, but I must remind you, no flash photography, as it may reveal this truly is just an illusion. Although when you leave this chapter believing I really did accomplish this miraculous endeavor, you must remember that no one could actually do such a thing.

Now that I have your attention ...

How, you may ask, do I plan on covering in a single chapter a topic like discipline that's had entire books written on it? I can honestly tell you I'm not sure. Many of you may have picked up this book hoping it was filled from cover to cover with discipline ideas and techniques. But as I said in the introduction, parenting is so much more than discipline, and I believe if you work to do all the other things in this book, your focus will change and your need for discipline will decrease.

I know the need to discipline our kids will never go away (that's why I kept one chapter on this). It's one thing loving parents do to help mold our little humans' basically evil nature into something that pleases God. But I don't believe that the majority of our interactions with our children should be focused on discipline, so I didn't focus the majority of this book on it either.

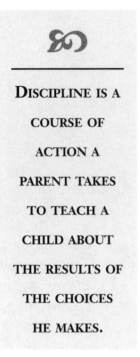

DISCIPLINE IS A COURSE OF ACTION A PARENT TAKES TO TEACH A CHILD ABOUT THE RESULTS OF THE CHOICES HE MAKES.

There are many good books that address discipline in great depth, and I'd encourage you to read those if you're truly struggling with the issue. But for the purpose of this book, I'll give you some basic suggestions and guidelines I hope you'll find helpful as you evaluate how effective your discipline is.

DISCIPLINE 101

I've chosen several basic components of effective discipline to cover in this chapter. I won't cover a slew of actual techniques for you to wade through and consider; instead, I'll focus on the theory behind the techniques—the root of effective discipline.

If the theory behind your chosen discipline technique is flawed, the technique won't be effective. You may feel the technique just doesn't work for your child. But before you throw out the technique, I'd suggest you look at the root of the problem. There are plenty of effective techniques, but none of them will work in the hands of ineffective parents.

This chapter will describe what *must* be present for whatever techniques you choose to be effective. Just about any parent will become more effective when these guidelines are understood and used.

Before we address the theories, let's define discipline. Are punishment and discipline the same thing? I don't believe so. Punishment is about placing pain in your child's life to reduce the likelihood of a given behavior occurring again. On the other hand, discipline focuses more on teaching than on pain. Discipline is a course of action a parent takes to teach a child about the results of the choices he makes.

Although the words *punishment* and *discipline* are often used interchangeably, I believe discipline is what parents are really after. We want our children to learn through experience, and we want that experience to curtail negative behavior. So as you move through this chapter, keep in mind that regardless which word we use, the focus is on teaching rather than on suffering.

We'll cover four specific parts of effective discipline.

RELATIONSHIPS BEFORE RULES

The most effective discipline occurs in an environment where there's already a relationship established on love and trust. Children want and seek the approval of people they love, and they learn early on that compliance and obedience often brings that approval. I'm not saying that our approval should be conditional (it shouldn't), but we all know that when our children do what we expect them to we should express approval.

However, if you haven't taken time to build a healthy, loving, and safe relationship with your children, they'll struggle with wanting to obey. If they believe that all you care about is their obedience, they'll likely begin to withhold it. Your child must feel and believe that he, not his obedience, is the most important thing to you.

Getting to really know your child will benefit both your relationship and your ability to discipline effectively. Take time to study your child. Get to know what makes him tick. Find out his likes and dislikes, what he deems important, and what motivates him. These bits of information will help your general interaction with him and help you determine when a behavior requires discipline. The better you know your child, the better you can distinguish between childish irresponsibility and willful defiance, and, therefore, the better you will respond. The more you work to get to know your child from the inside out, the stronger your relationship with him can be, and the more effective you can be in molding him into a healthy adult.

> **THE PARENTING TEAM'S ABILITY TO GO WITH THE FLOW AND MAKE ADJUSTMENTS MIDGAME IS AN ESSENTIAL SKILL.**

FLEXIBILITY IS KEY

Flexibility is a major component of building relationships before rules. Because your relationship with your child is always changing, you must be flexible enough to change with it. Just when you think you have your child and this parenting thing all figured out, the jungle changes. Some changes are gradual and minimal. But at other times—such as your child's "terrible twos" and adolescence—you may feel like you've been thrown into a whole new world.

As your relationship changes with your growing child, your techniques will also require adjustment along the way. The parenting techniques and consequences that worked when your child was a toddler or preschooler won't be effective when he's fifteen. Also, what worked well with one child may have no impact on another.

The parenting team's ability to go with the flow and make adjustments midgame is an essential skill to surviving the jungle that seems to be growing faster than you can keep up. If your interactions with your children are rigid, and you insist on keeping things just as they've always been and reacting the same with each child in every situation, you're probably headed for disaster. But if you embrace flexibility across situations, ages, and personalities, your parent-child relationship will grow deeper, even through discipline.

PARENTS WHO RESPOND INSTEAD OF REACT ARE MUCH LESS LIKELY TO HAVE TO BACKTRACK OR APOLOGIZE AFTER OVERREACTING OR OVERDISCIPLINING.

REACTING VS. RESPONDING

How you address your child's misbehavior can tell him whether the relationship or the rules are most important to you. One way this is evident is whether you react or respond when you're disciplining. Let's look at the difference.

Many parents discipline impulsively and reactively, acting almost on reflex. Without even thinking, they answer misbehavior with the first (often hurtful) words that come to mind and follow that with equally impulsive actions (usually more about your anger than your child's behavior).

Reactive parents spend lots of time back-peddling or apologizing because they may later find out additional information about a misbehavior situation that changes their whole view—and therefore what their response should have been. Reactive parents are most likely to be inconsistent, because their reaction is based in large part on their own feelings. One day they may be in a bad mood and react strongly to misbehavior; a couple of days later, they may be exhausted or in a great mood and let the same offense slide on by.

Finally, reactive parents often don't follow through with whatever they said while reacting. Because the response was impulsive and emotional, it was also likely to be irrational and unrealistic. These parents may have made threats and realized they would never see them through once they calmed down. Ignoring the offense altogether sends their children mixed and confusing messages.

> **YOU CAN'T EFFECTIVELY ENFORCE THE RULES IF THE RULES WERE NEVER EFFECTIVELY SET.**

On the other hand, there are responding parents who think before they take action. They take a moment (or several) to sort out the situation, get all the facts, and consider Junior's motivations for his actions before disciplining. They acknowledge their own emotions and reactions and wait for these to come under control before responding so they don't damage their relationship with their child. Parents who respond instead of react are much less likely to have to backtrack or apologize after overreacting or overdisciplining.

Parents who are responders are more concerned about the parent-child relationship than in simply seeing misbehavior as something that requires punishment. By taking time to sort out your own feelings and consider all the facts, you show your child you treasure him and want to respond appropriately and effectively.

SETTING APPROPRIATE RULES

Once you've established the relationship between you and your child, you can turn your attention to the rules. When many parents think of discipline, they think only about enforcing the rules. But you can't effectively enforce the rules if the rules were never effectively set.

If your children aren't clear on what the rules are, how can you enforce them? If speed-limit laws were never established and posted, no one could get a ticket. If a policeman pulled you over by for speeding, you'd probably argue openly, "No one told me what the limits were, so how could I know I was speeding? You can't give me a ticket!"

Our children will feel the same way if we try to discipline them for a misbehavior they never knew was wrong. Don't wait until a rule is broken to identify it as a rule, then punish whoever broke the invisible rule. Even Romans 4:15 tells us, "And where there is no law there is no transgression." If you don't take time to establish family rules, don't plan on disciplining your children.

Consider these pointers.

Rules should be limited in number. Rules communicate that something is important for your family's safety and welfare, and therefore they will be enforced every time they are broken. If your rule list is a mile long, not only will your children not be able to keep up with all of them, but you won't be able to enforce them consistently. So establish rules that will govern your family so they grow, not get weighed down by the sheer number of rules on your list.

It may help you limit your rules to consider the difference between rules, responsibilities, and respect. Rules are the "Thou shalt nots," behaviors parents deem unacceptable within the family and therefore are openly stated as requirements.

Responsibilities are daily-living issues, the activities that each family member shares some investment in getting accomplished, such as daily or weekly chores that keep the family and home running smoothly.

Finally, respect is how we define how we'll treat each other in our home. This category includes such things as manners, asking to borrow things, returning things that have been borrowed, how we speak to each other, and how we manage conflict.

If you notice your list of rules growing too long, check if you've been including items that better fall in the responsibility or respect categories. Responsibilities may also need to be clearly established, but may change from time to time and therefore shouldn't be part of the rules.

Rules should be clearly defined and understood. You can't simply make a list of rules and expect everyone to know what they mean. Sit down with your family and discuss the rules. Clearly define what each means until you feel comfortable that each family member understands it to the best of his or her ability. Vague or abstract concepts like honesty may need to be defined, and loopholes may need to be addressed. Does everyone in the family understand what "white lies" are, and have you addressed how these will be handled? Will the parents be held to the same set of rules? If not, why not? Will children of different ages be held to different levels of compliance until they reach a point of understanding? All these issues need to be addressed to be sure the rules are clearly and specifically communicated.

Rules should be written down and posted for all to see. Once again, God serves as our example: He made sure his rules were written and made visible. He knew we'd forget them, pretend to forget them, or try to change them if he didn't make sure they were there for all to read and re-read if necessary.

Once our rules have been established, discussed, and understood, it would serve us well to write them down and post them somewhere for future reference. That will help do away with the excuses "I forgot" or "That's not what I thought you said."

Rules should be enforced. If the rules were important enough to be established, clarified, and written down, they're important enough to be enforced. This is your parental responsibility and you mustn't shirk it. Too many parents today don't take on the responsibility of enforcing rules, and our society suffers because of it.

> **TOO MANY PARENTS TODAY DON'T TAKE ON THE RESPONSIBILITY OF ENFORCING RULES.**

It's helpful to determine the consequences for breaking the rules before they're ever broken. This information can easily be posted right along with the rules. Predetermined consequences let the child know before choosing an action what its results will be, often deterring him from making wrong choices and decreasing the need for discipline. Secondly, they help the parents respond quickly to misbehavior, because the consequence has already been established and they don't have to think it through every time.

I have one final note on setting appropriate rules. We all know we can't predict everything we'll encounter with our children, and when an established rule or responsibility is broken, there should be a consequence for that action. However, when a child misbehaves but didn't know the behavior was wrong, the response should be different. If no rule was established, the first offense should garner a rebuke or statement that the behavior is unacceptable. Then discuss what a more appropriate action would have been and if some sort of restitution may be necessary for the offense. A rule or standard of behavior should be set from that point forward.

BE SPECIFIC AND CONCRETE WHEN REQUESTING A BEHAVIOR FROM YOUR CHILD.

CLEAR AND SPECIFIC COMMUNICATION

DID YOU GET THE MESSAGE?

Communicating with children can be a challenge anytime, but it seems especially difficult around discipline issues. We must remember we're not dealing with little adults here. They don't think like us, understand words the same way we do, or view the world from our same perspective. Therefore we must learn to speak a language they can understand if we hope to get our messages through.

When we interact with our children, we need to remember that, for the most part, they're very concrete thinkers and vague/abstract meanings in phrases and words are often lost on them. This is especially important when discussing discipline. If you want your child to do what you say and avoid the consequences of noncompliance, find out if he even understood what you said. If your child never received the proper message, he can't comply, and you wouldn't be right in disciplining him for something he didn't even know he was supposed to do.

Telling a child to "be good in the store" is a vague statement that likely won't be received accurately. Concrete thinkers need concrete and measurable rules and directives to follow. Concrete things that can be seen, heard, touched, or observed in some way are likely to be measured the same way by most people. You can't observe "be good," and if you could, it would likely be defined differently by different people. But you can observe "walk beside me, and don't touch the things on the shelf." All those involved could agree if the directive had been broken.

IF YOU TELL YOUR CHILD NO OR TO STOP IN NO UNCERTAIN TERMS, HE NEEDS TO LEARN YOU MEAN BUSINESS.

Not everyone will define "clean your room" the same. But you are likely to get a strong consensus on "Put your books on the shelf and your clothes in your drawers."

In the Cherry household, when the children are told to go clean their rooms, they'll ask, "Is that Mommy clean or Daddy clean?" Our kids have learned Mom and Dad have two different standards of clean, and we all know what they mean. When we respond "Mommy clean," the moans go up; they each know that means much more than a walking path through the room. "Mommy clean" may seem vague and abstract to those of you who haven't lived in the Cherry home. But through many cooperative room cleanings, that term is now very concrete to our kids.

You may think your children know what you mean about similar phrases, but I caution you not to assume that. Ask them what they think you mean when you use a particular phrase such as "be good." Depending on their answer, you may or may not want to keep using it. But, in general, be specific and concrete when requesting a behavior from your child.

Here are some pointers to make sure you're giving clear messages:

1. Make eye contact with your child. Get on his level if at all possible and make sure you have his attention before instructing.

2. Eliminate distractions. Tell your kids what you expect of them at the store while you're still at home or sitting in your car. If you wait until you're in the store, you'll have too many distractions competing for your child's attention.

3. Be specific and clear both about the expected behavior and the consequences that can be expected for noncompliance.

4. Ask your child questions to make sure your message was received.

For discipline to be effective, parents must learn to stop repeating themselves. If you've learned to communicate clearly and you know your children are receiving your message, you don't need to keep repeating that message or give your children a million and one chances to comply with your command before you intervene with discipline. If you tell your child no or to stop in no uncertain terms, he needs to learn you mean business.

When you tell your child no and he continues to beg, plead, whine, bribe and bargain, or ignore your statements, don't keep giving more chances. All he should hear from you is "I've already answered that question and I'm not going to answer it again." Then ignore continued efforts.

If a child is told to do or stop doing something, he should *not* be "reminded" over and over or given half a dozen warnings and threats. He should be told once, followed by a brief (five to ten seconds) pause to look for compliance. If he complies, he should be praised for doing what he was told. If he isn't complying, he should be given one (and only one) reminder or warning; something like, "Tommy, if you don't _____ (statement of what he's expected to do) _____, you will have to _____ (statement of the consequence) _____." Wait just a few seconds again for compliance. If Tommy does what he's supposed to, praise him; if not, implement the consequence. No more chances.

This teaches a child not only to do what he's told but to do it immediately. When you communicate like this you don't wear yourself out giving multiple warnings but let yourself respond quickly before you're tired and angry. Everyone does better.

Unfortunately, I see many parents wearing themselves out giving a child chance after chance to comply and never applying a consequence until they've literally reached the end of their rope and do so out of anger and frustration.

Jim and I were feeling adventurous one Saturday afternoon and decided to tackle one of the most dangerous parenting obstacles known to man: McDonald's Playplace. The kids practically swallowed their cheeseburgers whole so they could move on to more important things, like climbing through two-story tunnels. As Jim and I sat finishing our meal, we observed one mom and her futile efforts to get little Jordan to leave the restaurant.

Her first maneuver was to yell several times for "Jordy" in the general direction of the tunnels. If Jordy was in the tunnels, I'm not sure he could have heard his mother over the racket of twenty-five or thirty other kids yelling just as loud. But his mother continued to bellow out his name, a little louder and more passionately each time. I was just about to decide that Jordy didn't exist when a little, sandy-blond bundle of boy about five came sliding out of the tunnel. His mother immediately greeted him and began her next set of maneuvers. She openly scolded Jordy for not coming when she called him. When he said he never heard her calling, she simply told him he should have been listening and that it was time to go.

Those seemed to be fighting words and Jordy immediately began pleading for "just one more time, please?"

"No, we don't have time." she replied.

"But Mommy, you said if I ate all my lunch I could play. I didn't get to play in the ball pit. I just went down the tunnel. Please can I play just a little longer?"

I noticed Mom's shoulders drop as she gave in, "OK, but just for a couple more minutes."

Before long, Mom was back to yelling for Jordy again. This time it was "really time to go," and he was to come out and get his shoes on "right now!" When Jordy didn't respond right away, Mom got up and went to the ball pit to call him out. She continued to yell, but now she made eye contact and gave an intimidating glare—and for a little extra punch, she called him "Jordan Allen."

Jordan Allen was having more fun than he knew what to do with and it seemed to be affecting his body. He'd look in Mom's direction when she called and even respond with something like, "OK, I'm coming"—but then his little legs just wouldn't seem to move toward the exit. He did seem to be able to jump up out of the balls, then go tumbling back into a sea of polka dots.

Mom was becoming more and more frustrated and changed her strategy altogether. This time, in a fairly normal tone of voice (at least to start with) she told Jordy that he had until she counted to three to get out of that ball pit "or else." Have you ever really wondered what "else" is? I'm sure Jordy did, but it couldn't have concerned him too much because he didn't respond.

"Jordy, I mean it! I'm going to count to three; now get out of there."

Brief pause.

"OK, I guess you want me to start counting don't you?"

Pause. No Jordy.

"Fine, if that's the way you want it ... "

By this time I wanted to yell, *"Start counting already!"* or do it for her. I couldn't believe what I was seeing. Before she even starting counting, she gave Jordy several warnings. No wonder this mom looked exhausted; she was wearing herself out.

"One!"

Finally! I was relieved to learn Mom actually did know how to count, but quickly that relief was gone. Counting to three may sound easy to most of us, but here's how an ineffective parent counts to three.

"I said one; did you hear me?"

"Two."

"Jordy, stop ignoring me, I know you can hear me."

"I'm already at two; do you want me to keep going?"

"Two-and-a-half."

"Jordan Allen ... I'm going to say three and you know what that means."

"If I have to come in there and get you, you will get a spanking."

"I don't want to have to say three ... so get out here right now."

"Two-and-three-quarters."

"This is your last chance."

"Three." And with that little Jordy is emerging from the ball pit. As far as I could tell, the "else" he was threatened with was never given. He was, however, grabbed by the arm and dragged to the shoe shelf, being lectured all the way about how he never minds. The battle didn't end there; it continued over tying the shoes, getting his coat on, and throwing away his trash. I won't bore you with the details, but I bet you can guess how it went.

As that mom and son left McDonald's that day, neither one appeared happy. What could have been a fun outing together had turned very sour, and I felt sorry for them both. As I was thinking about how this could have gone differently, Jim smiled at me and said, "It's time to go. Who wants to call the kids out of the tunnels?"

Understanding and Allowing Consequences

The final important aspect of effective discipline is allowing your child to experience the consequences of his actions. In the McDonald's story above, we witnessed a mom who appeared largely ineffective because she seemed either unwilling to let Jordy experience the consequences of his disobedience or unable to give an effective consequence. I guess some would argue Jordy did suffer a consequence: He had to endure his mother yelling and lecturing. I'd have to disagree. The purpose of a consequence is to curb a child's behavior. What this mom did in no way seemed to change Jordy's behavior. No appropriate consequence was set in motion; therefore, no effective discipline took place.

I reiterate: If rules are important enough to be established, they should be important enough to be enforced. It's our job as parents to mold our children's behavior through the rules we establish and the consequences we apply.

If we refuse to apply consequences, our children will never

learn what behavior is appropriate and what isn't. If we think we're helping our kids by protecting them from the pain of their poor choices, we need to think again! We can't protect them forever, and eventually they'll move away from our protection into the real world. The real world doesn't care about protecting your child from pain; it cares whether people obey the rules and act responsibly. If your child didn't already learn that, the pain may be huge then. So, when you're considering bailing your child out of some consequence he deserves, reconsider if this pain is better experienced now or later when it may be bigger.

CONSEQUENCES ARE FOR BOTH GOOD AND BAD BEHAVIOR

To help you become more comfortable with enforcing consequences in your child's life, it may help to realize you're likely already allowing some consequences—positive ones. If you can see the value of positive consequences, it's not a big leap to seeing the benefits of negative ones as well.

WITHOUT A NEGATIVE OUTCOME TO A POOR CHOICE, THERE'S NO REASON FOR YOUR CHILD TO STOP MAKING THAT CHOICE.

A consequence is *any* action that's a result of a particular behavior or choice. It's closely tied to the principle of "every action has a reaction." Our chosen behaviors cause both positive and negative outcomes, and outcomes that determine how likely it is we'll engage in that same behavior again in the future. If we like the consequence, we're more likely to do the same thing again than if we don't like the consequence. If your goal as a parent is to bend your child's behavior in a direction that will be productive and effective when she's an adult, applying consequences is one of your best tools.

Positive choices usually bring positive consequences, such as rewards, praise, and compliments. These reinforce your child's good behavior and, when applied, increase the chances of that behavior being repeated. Many parents are good at this part of consequences. We love to praise our kids. We're usually pretty good at rewarding good behavior, outstanding performance, good grades, and responsibility with words, money, and physical touch. We feel good about ourselves when we're applying positive consequences—but we usually don't when the consequences are negative.

Negative behaviors or noncompliance usually cause negative consequences—paying for something you broke, loosing a privilege, or receiving a spanking. When applied correctly and consistently, negative consequences will reduce the chances of your child engaging in that misbehavior again. We'd all claim our goal is to help our children stop behaving inappropriately, but we often slack off on the one thing that will help them— negative consequences. If we refuse to discipline our child's disobedience, we must resolve ourselves to their continuing to disobey. Without a negative outcome to a poor choice, there's no reason for your child to stop making that choice.

Many parents avoid applying negative consequences to their child's misbehavior because of how it makes *them* feel. "I feel like a rotten parent when I take the PlayStation away." Well I'm here to tell you if you don't, you're likely to feel worse when your child grows up and doesn't understand the importance of responsibilities.

None of us likes to make our children mad. We hate it when little Tommy tells us we're "mean." But to be an effective parent, you need to look beyond the here and now into the future. Your child doesn't see the big picture, but you can. Being a good parent means teaching your children any of their actions can have consequences, not just the positive ones. You'll feel like a good parent when you see your child learn to respond appropriately because you effectively applied both positive and negative consequences.

PARENTING IN PRACTICE

OUT OF THE MOUTHS OF BABES

This is one of the riskiest assignments I'll ever give. Before you do it, brace yourself for the outcome and be ready to accept what you hear. Your task is to sit down with your child and ask him, on a scale of one to ten, "How much do you feel loved and treasured by me?"

Based on what you hear, you may want to follow that up with something like, "How could I improve that score?" You may want this to become a regular, periodic check-in to see how you're doing. Wouldn't it be great if you did this after a difficult time between you and your child, and you still received a fairly high score? When our kids experience that we love them even when things aren't going great, we have succeeded.

CHAPTER 14

AND YOU CAN'T MAKE ME!

The Art of Managing Power Struggles

THE YOUNGEST WARRIOR

The opportunity for a battle of the wills starts by the time a child is around twelve months old—even younger for some. In our home, we noticed what seemed like power struggles from the age of three weeks old with our oldest child, Taffeta. I'd just started my psychology internship when Jim and I found out I was pregnant. We'd been married five years and, as much as we each wanted a baby, we'd been focused on preventing that blessing from entering our life just yet. When people (mainly prospective grandmas) would ask if we were ever going to have kids, Jim would respond, "We're having a PhD instead." Well, at least that was the plan.

The last step of birthing that PhD was the one-year internship. We could see the light at the end of the tunnel and were turning our minds toward starting a family. We knew we couldn't have a baby during the internship—that would simply be a disaster. You don't take time off during that intense year, especially not an eight-week maternity leave. But we were sure we could time things perfectly to finish the year and the PhD and then have the baby. Sounds great, doesn't it?

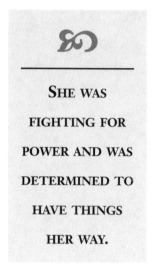

SHE WAS FIGHTING FOR POWER AND WAS DETERMINED TO HAVE THINGS HER WAY.

I know some of you are already laughing—two young, excited, unaware people thinking they can continue to keep their life right on track and plan when pregnancy and birth will fit into their schedule. Well, this was no laughing matter (at least not at the time).

We did some research, talked to several people (especially prospective grandmas), and were generally assured it was "sure to take several months" to get pregnant. If we wanted to "plan" a baby to be born in thirteen months, we'd better "get off birth control now, get it out of your system, and allow your body time to prepare to get pregnant, because it doesn't just happen the first month."

Well, we took all their good advice, and I'm here to tell you *they were all wrong!* Two weeks after stopping the pill, I was pregnant. When we actually figured this out, panic set in. We were sure the PhD that we'd been trying to have for years was about to slip right through our fingers.

I was terrified to tell my supervisor I was going to need to take time off. I was sure she'd say I'd have to quit my internship and reapply next year, but she didn't. She agreed to work with me by letting me work extra before the baby arrived and after my return to complete the required hours. I was thrilled, but it meant only four weeks of maternity leave. At the time, I thought that would be no big deal and agreed.

That brings us to the first power struggle. Our precious, innocent little redhead arrived at the end of May and captured our hearts. Things were going really well for about two weeks, and then I started thinking about the fact that in two more weeks, I wouldn't be here with her every moment of her day. Although that was hard to consider, I'd been preparing myself for it for months. The hard part was that if I wasn't there she would have to learn to take a bottle. With that realization, the fight was on.

Of course, I didn't like the idea much myself. Those feeding times had become a special time for Mom and Daughter to snuggle, sing, and bond. I didn't want to give it up. But Taffeta quickly decided she simply wasn't going to give it up. She knew what she wanted and had no intention of it changing.

Now, can I tell you that she was consciously aware of her choices and what she was doing? Of course not. But from our point of view, she was fighting for power and was determined to have things her way. She could cry and scream and fight against that bottle so long and hard that her loving parents would eventually give in. After all, "She has to eat, doesn't she?" We couldn't let her go hungry, so we'd take the bottle away and let her have what she wanted, and amazingly she would calm down, eat well, and sleep like an angel. How would I ever go back to work knowing she wouldn't eat while I was gone?

We kept trying, unsuccessfully of course, for about a week, and by then the panic had really set in. We only had a few more days left until either our child would start starving to death or I would have to quit my job. (Yes, our thought process was a bit extreme.) It was time to call in the special troops—Grandma! (After all, it was at least partly her fault we were even in this predicament.)

I called my mom and cried on the phone. I explained Taffeta simply wouldn't take a bottle, and I had tried everything. I could almost hear her smiling on the other end of the phone. She said she'd be right there. They lived about an hour away, but at least I knew help was on the way, and we all started to relax a bit. I had no idea how Grandma would really help, because, after all, I had tried everything—but at least she'd be there and give her support.

When Grandma arrived, she grabbed little Taffeta up in her arms and snuggled with her. "So I hear you've been giving your mama and daddy some trouble, little one. What's that all about? Haven't you learned yet that, as much as you may want to be, you really aren't the one in charge here?" I remember thinking my mom had gone mad. Did she think that talking and reasoning with a three-week-old baby would fix this problem? Maybe I had called the wrong person.

For about the next half hour, Grandma did nothing but play. Taffeta started to fuss at one point and I knew it was time for her to eat. I asked my mom what the plan was, and she just smiled and said, "All in good time; just be patient. She isn't *really* hungry yet." Who did she think she was telling me my daughter wasn't "really hungry yet"? I'm her mama and I think I know if she's hungry or not! But Jim reminded me we'd called and asked for her help, so we should let her do it her way. We both knew our way wasn't working.

About fifteen minutes later, Taffeta really started to fuss and Grandma finally asked for the bottle. By the time I had warmed it and handed it to her, Taffeta was pitching a fit. "Mom, she really hates this thing. I don't think she'll take it at all now that she's so upset. Why don't I feed her a little and calm her down, and then you can try?"

"She's fine, Debbie. Why don't you and Jim just go for a walk or something and come back in a little while?"

"Are you nuts? You have no idea what you're getting into here. You're going to need me in just a few minutes. I'll just hang out in the living room. I don't want her going hungry. You can try for a few minutes, but if it doesn't work, I'll just feed her."

Mom just shook her head and said, "Have it your way, but I promise you Taffeta will be fine. It's going to be much harder on you to hear her cry. If you want me to do this, you have to agree to stay out of the nursery unless I call for you."

I very reluctantly agreed, only because I knew she'd be calling for me soon.

Grandma and Taffeta headed off to the "Showdown Corral" while Mom and Dad stood right outside the nursery door. I could just barely hear my mom over the baby's screams. She was talking in a normal, loving tone of voice, telling Taffeta that she loved her. "Hey there, pretty girl, it's time to take this bottle. Your mama has to go back to work in a few days, and if you don't want to go hungry, you'll have to like this thing." There she goes with that talking and reasoning thing again. I'm really beginning to wonder how her four children turned out so great if this is how she parented.

The more Mom talked, the more intense Taffeta's crying became. It was as if she understood what her grandma was saying and was responding with a loud, "No way! Not as long as I'm in charge!" But Taffeta had met her match. Grandma continued rocking and reasoning with this out-of-control child, "And besides, you really don't have a choice on this one. You're not in charge here. You can fight this all you want, but eventually you'll get hungry enough that you'll eat, and I'll just keep rocking you until you do."

POWER STRUGGLES CAN AND DO ERUPT AT ANY AND ALL AGES AND STAGES OF CHILD DEVELOPMENT.

I was totally beside myself and started to bust through the door and rescue my daughter from this ogre. I made it far enough to peek around the door frame before Jim grabbed me and pulled me back. That was just close enough for me to hear my mom start singing to Taffeta, "I'm more stubborn than you are. I'm more stubborn than you."

And I finally got it. This wasn't about Taffeta starving or not. This was about Taffeta wanting what she wanted and doing her best to get it. It was the first of many battles for who's in charge. All that talking and reasoning my mom was doing wasn't for Taffeta at all. It was teaching and reminding her parents that they needed to be the ones in charge. They needed to be parents.

I have no idea how long the showdown continued, because Jim and I left the house and went for a drive. We knew we were leaving Taffeta in good hands that loved her enough not to allow her to be in charge at three weeks old. We learned a big lesson and Taffeta learned to take a bottle.

> YOU CAN AVOID MANY IMPENDING CONFLICTS BY SIMPLY LEARNING TO GIVE YOUR CHILD CHOICES, WHICH GIVES HER A SENSE OF CONTROL.

WHEN DO POWER STRUGGLES START?

As we begin the parenting process, many of us make the wrong assumption that the fight for control begins when they hit their teens—probably because those battles are the ones we hear other parents talking about the most. Those seem to be the "biggies." But power struggles can and do erupt at any and all ages and stages of child development. Your child may not have started fighting for control as young as ours did, but I know she'll start long before she becomes a teenager.

The foundation for the power struggles during the teen years is actually built when the child is much younger. Children begin trying to control their world and the people around them at a very young age, and how we handle those seemingly minor (and maybe even a little "cute" at times) issues of who's in charge will set the stage for the more tumultuous years to come.

WHY MUST WE BATTLE?

Power struggles at any age arise because there's a *naturally* occurring clash between the parents' needs and responsibilities and the child's desires. The parent is trying to guide, influence, and control the child, while the child wants to be in control of her own decisions, actions, and life.

When these two forces collide (and they do so often) the earth (or at least the home) may quake and rifts may appear between the parties involved. When all's said and done and the quake is over, no one is glad it happened. Everyone is overly emotional, hurt, and exhausted. Power struggles can be quite destructive. And although we can't completely avoid these impending disasters, we can take some precautions to limit their occurrence and cut down significantly on the damage they cause.

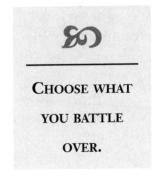

CHOOSE WHAT YOU BATTLE OVER.

We know there will be power struggles; wouldn't it be nice if we could choose where and when these occur? The contest for power will seem almost constant for most parents by the time their baby reaches two, and it doesn't stop until your child leaves home (maybe even longer). If you don't want to be in a constant state of conflict with your child, you'll need to choose your battles carefully—to learn when to fight and when not to.

Children start wanting to exert some control over their own lives around two years old—what's come to be known as the "terrible twos." You can avoid many impending conflicts by simply learning to give your child choices, which gives her a sense of control. When she can choose between picking up her toys now or after lunch, drinking milk or juice for breakfast, wearing her red or green dress, or listening to music or reading a book for quiet time, she feels in charge of her life. When she has a choice of *how* to do something, she's less likely to need to *prove* to you that she will or will not actually do it. When you let her make as many decisions as possible for herself, she won't feel obligated to prove that she can make decisions. Letting her make age-appropriate decisions both builds her sense of self-esteem and decreases the number of power struggles.

Another way to decrease the number and strength of power struggles is to choose what you battle over. Many parents struggle with knowing when to back away from an issue. We think we always know what's best for our children and tend to want things done our way (maybe that's where our kids learned it). This "all-knowing" mindset will set you up for many battles.

Many of the issues parents and kids fight over are really insignificant in the big picture. Keeping her room clean, how loud she plays her music, and when she can start shaving her legs aren't moral or spiritual issues that will damage her future. Yet many parents are fighting tooth and nail to get their way, and kids will fight just as hard right back to get theirs. Is it really worth fighting over a hair style, eating all her green beans, or simply proving you're right?

There will be plenty of battles that do have long-term results, involve moral issues, or could be dangerous to your child. You have a better chance of her listening to you over these topics if you haven't caused her to go selectively deaf from the constant battle of the wills over less significant issues.

THE POWER-STRUGGLE SHUFFLE

As you raise your children and maneuver through the inevitable power struggles, you may feel like you've been asked to dance the jig while walking on eggshells through a minefield. (How's that for a word picture?) You have to keep moving, but may feel you could slip and fall at any moment or if you make one wrong move, you could set off World War III in your own home. As impossible as this feat may feel, a few tactics you can learn will help tremendously. Let's learn the steps to the power-struggle dance.

MOVE ONTO THE DANCE FLOOR

Our human desire for social interactions with others sets the stage for the dance. If we never interacted with anyone else, there would be no power struggles. We'd simply go about our business, doing what we wanted to do and dancing to our own music. But that's not how life works. When we want to interact with others, we move onto the dance floor. As we do, we become immediately aware others on the dance floor seem to have their own ideas about how this should be done. We may agree with some more than others, but we won't agree with anyone all the time. That's when a power-struggle dance begins.

MAY I HAVE THIS DANCE?

As two (or more) people move toward each other from

opposite directions, one of them begins the power-struggle dance with a simple request. You know you've been asked to dance when you realize the two of you have different opinions on an issue that's been presented. These invitations to dance can come from either parent or child and may sound something like:

DON'T BE AFRAID TO TAKE CHARGE AND STAY IN CHARGE ON MORAL, ETHICAL, SPIRITUAL, AND PHYSICAL-SAFETY TOPICS.

"I told you to turn your radio down! I'm not going to tell you again!"

"I think I'm ready to start shaving my legs."

"You'll sit here until you eat all your dinner."

"I'm not going to church this morning."

"You will take your medicine right now!"

"I don't want to wear a coat!"

"You will be home by eleven o'clock."

However it comes out, the invitation has been made, and the issue has been presented. The dance is on.

I WANT TO LEAD!

As the dancers take their places and lock arms in position, the disagreement about who's in charge begins. Both parties believe they know the best way to move about the dance floor as smoothly as possible. Each is sure they need to be the one leading the way. But as they fight for control, they look anything but smooth. The partners are doing more pushing and shoving than gliding and sliding. This battle takes lots of energy and eventually will wear the partners completely out if something isn't done to change the music they're dancing to.

This is your turn as the parents to really shine. You'll be able to strut your stuff by evaluating the situation and choosing the dance's future direction. Depending on the music playing, you can choose any of the next three steps.

Step up. Decide very early on if this is a dance that you must lead on. If that's the case, step forward, assume the lead, and don't let go. There are some power-struggle topics a parent should and must stand firm in. Don't be afraid to take charge and stay in charge on moral, ethical, spiritual, and physical-safety topics.

Step back. More often than parents may like, the music that's playing doesn't require us to take the lead. In situations that don't fall in the categories above, your best bet may be to step back and let your child take the lead. Just because you're the parent doesn't mean you always have to lead the dance. Allowing your child to be in charge of the when, where, and how for much of the dance gives them a sense of power and control they're desperately searching for.

Many times your best step is a step back. Step back, take a deep breath, and take time to think, listen, and evaluate the situation. Once you do, you may realize you as the parent couldn't control this situation even if you wanted to. You can't force your child to eat, go to sleep, and be happy, so why try? You may also realize this is a situation your child is completely capable of handling. Or, you may decide it's a good time for your child to try her best and experience either the rewards or consequences that result.

Another way you may step back is by deciding not to dance at all right now. As you evaluate the situation, you may become aware dancing right now won't work for anyone involved. Maybe everyone is hungry, tired, rushed, or just plain cranky. You may do everyone a favor by just stepping off the dance floor and getting something to eat, getting to bed, or slowing down. Choosing not to dance in these situations is stepping back and postponing the confrontation (at least for a while).

Step Over. Sometimes the music requires neither you nor your child to be completely in charge. In these situations, it might do both parties good to try to see things from the other's perspective. As you step over to your child's point of view, you may better understand the issue at hand. We parents often just decide we know what's best for our children or, even worse, just decide we want things our way. There may or may not be any good reason for our decision other than it's our decision.

> REMEMBER THAT GOD CREATED THIS LITTLE TREASURE, AND SEARCH TO FIND THE PEARLS YOU KNOW ARE WITHIN.

We need to learn our children won't always like what we like, want to do the same things we want to, or want to do things the same way we do. When the music playing is based on reasonable individual differences, we need to consider negotiation and compromise as the next step.

This is the step of choosing your battles. Many issues that we tend to fight to the death over really aren't life-and-death issues. Coming up with acceptable choices and alternatives to choose from that can lead to a win-win solution will eliminate the battle for control. Hearing a child's reasoning for why she wants to cut her hair or what activities he wants to participate in, then having them hear yours, will go far in reducing power struggles in your home.

PARENTING IN PRACTICE

TREASURE HUNTING

What do you think it would be like to go on an actual treasure hunt? I'm sure the journey would be exciting and sometimes exhausting. You'd likely spend time digging through dirt and rock as you're searching for the treasure you're sure is there somewhere. Then when you find it, I'm sure you'd want to shout it from the rooftops and let the whole world know.

Raising kids is kind of like that. We're on a hunt for buried treasure. It will be exciting at times and exhausting at times, but we'll continue to search for the treasure that lies within each of our kids. As you dig through the rock and rubble of difficult times with your children, take a minute to look for the good in your child. Remember that God created this little treasure, and search to find the pearls you know are within. Then when you find them, be sure to tell both your child and the world around you about the treasure you found.

CHAPTER 15

THE TREASURE OF PARENTING

A Few Final Words

℘

As we conclude this book, I'd like to take the last chapter to encourage you. The parenting jungle can be rough and full of traps, but the blessings we get from our years in this survival game are countless. Our children can drive us to the brink of insanity and challenge us in ways we never thought possible—but by the end of it all, we've grown just as much as they have, and they've taught us much about life and living it to the fullest. They truly are treasures from heaven.

I pray I've given you some new ideas you can begin implementing in your home immediately. I hope you've been encouraged to believe you can move through these difficult years with skills that can effectively grow your children to be all God intended them to be.

Most of all, I hope you understand parenting is a growing process for all involved. It may be easy before you're a parent yourself to think, "Oh, that parenting thing can't be all that hard." But when I became a parent myself, I learned that this thing called parenting is probably harder than anything else I had ever done. I learned there is no one answer that will work in every situation for every child. Nothing is cut and dried, and no amount of book knowledge can prepare you for every challenge or keep you from falling into one of the many traps you'll face every day.

As parents, we need to support and encourage each other, to keep trying until we find what works for each of our children. I hope we'll share ideas and suggestions that have worked for us with others who may be struggling. As we do, I pray we'll add, "Just give this a try and see how it works."

I know there are general parenting tactics that are effective with most kids in many different situations, but there's no definitive parenting style or skill that works all the time. As parents, we need to do the best we can to learn good parenting skills and implement them consistently. But even more than that, we need to be patient with ourselves and our children as we travel through this jungle we call the parenting years.

We're all human and need to accept that fact. There are no perfect parents or perfect kids—and when you place imperfect children in a home with imperfect parents, you'll have some mistakes. It's how you go about handling those mistakes, learning from them and changing things in the future, that can make the parenting process go much more smoothly.

Accept you have and will make mistakes. If you're willing to take responsibility for those mistakes and seek forgiveness, you'll teach your children to do the same as they make mistakes. Accepting our humanity will have a bigger impact on the parenting process and our long-term relationships with our children than any technique I could ever teach.

So as we bring this book to a close, I hope to leave you with hope and encouragement. As difficult as raising children can be at times, the blessings and rewards far outweigh the struggles.

Through these little treasures, we have the opportunity to become better people ourselves. Our children can teach us some very valuable life lessons if we'll take time to focus on our relationship with them. They can keep us young, remind us to slow down and play, help us see the beauty and humor in the world around us, inspire us to be better people, and bring us closer to God.

I know it wasn't until after I became a parent that I truly began to grasp the depth of love God could have for me. As I demonstrated love, forgiveness, and unconditional acceptance to my own children, God would often whisper in my ear, "That's how I love you, too." What a wonderful feeling to know that as we teach our children, we're being taught by God ourselves. That, I believe, is the true joy that comes when we are focused on "Escaping the Parent Trap."

READERS' GUIDE

*for Personal Reflection or
Group Discussion*

Readers' Guide

എ

Each of us who chooses to have children must learn to maneuver our way through the parenting jungle. It will be filled with wonderful times we'll remember all our lives—and difficult and draining times that will serve as trials to grow us stronger. *Escaping the Parent Trap* was written to give you a map to help you search for and find the wonderful blessings within each of your children. It was also written to provide guidance and instructions to help get both you and your children safely through the more treacherous parts of your jungle.

As you read the book, we hope you'll use the following study guide to help you dig a little deeper into the topics presented. As you work to personalize the information and apply it to your own personal parenting situation, you'll be better able to see the treasures both within your child and within the parenting process itself. You'll begin to focus on how to best grow your children into what God intends them to be. Helping your children reach their full potential and watching them blossom as they grow is truly a treasure of parenting.

Introduction
Parenting, a.k.a. "Survival of the Fittest"

1. How far into your marriage did you enter the "parenting jungle"? Did you feel prepared when it happened?

2. What was each of your reactions to finding out you were about to be parents? What did you do to start preparing?

3. What part or stage of parenting has been the most difficult for you so far?

4. What were some of your major adjustments once kids arrived? How did life change for you?

5. What would you include in a "Parenting Survival Kit"?

6. What, in your opinion, is the most important aspect of raising children?

Chapter 1: Train Up a Child
The Basics of Healthy Parenting

1. What are the two main parts of parenting described in Deuteronomy 6:6–9?

2. What's the difference between "training" and "teaching"?

3. Why is it important for a parent to "observe the commands of the Lord"?

4. Identify and discuss the three things parents must do to adequately teach and train their children.

5. How would you describe your "coaching" style? Do you send kids out there unprepared, prepared, or don't send them out at all?

6. Do you agree kids should experience consequences of their choices while still at home? Why or why not?

Chapter 2: And the Two Shall Be One
Being a Good Parenting Team

1. Evaluate you own self-esteem by writing down as many things as you can that you like about yourself. How did you do? Can you share three of them with the group?

2. What are you and your spouse doing to keep your marriage a priority? If nothing, what can you start doing this week? (Use the list of suggestions in the chapter to get you started.)

3. How, in your opinion, can a husband and wife help each other in parenting? How can they hinder each other?

4. What are you and your spouse's strengths and weaknesses as a co-parenting team?

5. How do the two of you handle parenting and discipline disagreements?

CHAPTER 3: YOU ARE MY SUNSHINE
LEARNING TO TREASURE YOUR CHILD

1. What does each letter of TREASURE stands for?

2. Of the eight components of TREASURE, which do you feel you are doing best in giving to your children? Which do you struggle with the most?

3. How have you noticed your physical touch has helped your child?

4. Do you shield and protect your child from things that can be harmful (such as what they watch, listen to, and read)? Is your level of protection appropriate, or would it be considered overprotection?

5. What is the Golden Rule for showing love to your kids? Do you know how your children give and receive love?

6. Do you agree that establishing boundaries for your children shows them that you treasure them?

CHAPTER 4: DO YOU LIKE YOU AS MUCH AS I LIKE YOU?
BUILDING YOUR CHILD'S SELF-ESTEEM

1. How healthy do you feel your children's self-esteem is?

2. Do you believe you can "overindulge" your child in praise?

3. What spoken or unspoken expectations do you hold for your child? Are they realistic?

4. Do you struggle with accepting your children's unique qualities? How can you help your children do better with accepting their differences?

5. How do you celebrate your children?

Chapter 5: A Child Spells Love T-I-M-E
Understanding the Power of
Quality and Quantity Time

1. Before reading this chapter, did you believe quality time or quantity time was best for your child? Now what do you believe?

2. Have you applied the quality vs. quantity argument to your own family to help you excuse your lack of time with your kids?

3. When you wrote down your top five priorities, what did you find? Did anything surprise or concern you?

4. How much time do you actually spend each day/week with your children? How do you think that measures up to what they need?

5. How good are you doing at budgeting your time? Is your schedule too full? What are you willing to do about it?

CHAPTER 6: MONKEY SEE, MONKEY DO
THE POWER OF MODELING

1. What reaction did you have as you read the opening story? Do you believe this could have been a real-life story?

2. Do you agree with the statement "Children do as they see, not as they are told?" Why or why not?

3. If kids model everything, why do you think we only notice them modeling our negative traits and not our positive ones?

4. Share a story (funny or otherwise) about when you noticed your child imitating you or another adult role model.

5. What behaviors has God revealed to you that you may need to change for your actions to match your words?

6. What do you believe your kids are learning about marriage by watching you and your spouse?

CHAPTER 7: I DON'T KNOW HOW I FEEL!
HELPING YOUR CHILD UNDERSTAND
AND EXPRESS FEELINGS

1. Are you comfortable with the expression of emotions in your home? If not, which ones make you uncomfortable?

2. Why do you believe God gave us our feelings? What purpose do they serve?

3. Do you believe anger is a sin? Why or why not?

4. How were emotions dealt with in your home growing up? Do you think that was a healthy learning experience?

5. How have you taught, allowed, and encouraged the full range of emotions to be expressed in your home?

6. What alternative expressions do you give your kids to replace inappropriate emotional expressions?

CHAPTER 8: CHILDREN OF VIRTUE
THE ART OF INSTILLING VALUES INTO YOUR CHILDREN

1. How old to you think a child has to be before we can start teaching values? Why?

2. What virtues do you hope to instill in your kids? How are you teaching those?

3. What three Scripture references did Dr. Cherry use to determine what values we should teach our children? Do you agree these should be our first priority? What others might you add?

4. Would you say that your life shows the virtues of honesty, gratitude, and respect?

5. Which virtue are you struggling with the most with your children?

CHAPTER 9: DO YOU HEAR WHAT I HEAR?
LEARNING TO COMMUNICATE WITH YOUR CHILD

1. On a scale from 1 to 10, how would you rate your general communication with your kids?

2. Do you really believe your children want to talk to you? Do you think your children believe you really want to talk to them?

3. Do you do more talking or listening when interacting with your children?

4. Of the five suggestions to being a better listener, which do you need to work on the most?

5. Are you a conversation choker or conversation nourisher? How can you become a better nourisher?

CHAPTER 10: BUT YOU ASKED ME
IF I WANTED TO AND I DON'T
PARENTING ISN'T POLITE

1. Do you believe parents should be polite? Should parents use "please" when expecting a child to do something? Why or why not?

2. Should a child be punished for saying no to a request? What about to a command?

3. Share a time when you noticed your child didn't understand what was meant by an adult concept or phrase.

4. Have you struggled with the issue of making requests when you meant it to be a command? What about the other way around— have you made commands you really meant to be requests? How did you handle these miscommunications?

5. When are appropriate times for choices? When should commands be used instead?

CHAPTER 11: THE BIG NO-NOS OF PARENTING
FOUR THINGS TO AVOID AT ALL COST

1. What types of boundaries or limits have you placed around your children? How have your children tested these boundaries?

2. What are "The Four Big No-Nos" of parenting? Why do you think they should be avoided?

3. Which of the four big no-nos are you most likely to fall prey to?

4. What's the difference between having a lack of follow-through or follow-up?

5. What do you believe is the long-term effect of making idle threats?

6. Do your children know how long they can wait before obeying you? How long do you think that is?

CHAPTER 12: THE POWER TOOLS OF PARENTING ATTENTION AND IGNORING

1. What are the power tools of parenting?

2. What other tools have you tried to use in parenting your kids? How well did they work?

3. How do you see your children grabbing for your attention? Are their efforts successful? Are they met more with positive attention, negative attention, or being ignored?

4. How do you feel about using ignoring as a major parenting tool? Why?

5. How can positive attention, negative attention, and ignoring actually change a child's behavior?

CHAPTER 13: THE INS AND OUTS OF EFFECTIVE DISCIPLINE LEARNING WHAT WILL REALLY WORK

1. What's the difference between discipline and punishment? Which do you use most?

2. A common saying about discipline is that "rules without relationship lead to rebellion." Do you agree with this statement? Why or why not?

3. How does focusing on building your relationship with your child help you be a more effective parent?

4. How have your discipline techniques changed over the years? What currently works for you?

5. What types of rules have you established for your home? Have you kept to the guidelines mentioned in the chapter?

6. Describe some positive and negative consequences. How does allowing consequences impact a child's behavior?

CHAPTER 14: AND YOU CAN'T MAKE ME! THE ART OF MANAGING POWER STRUGGLES

1. How early did power struggles between parent and child start happening in your home? What do you remember about those early battles?

2. Why do power struggles occur? Can they be decreased or eliminated completely? If so, how?

3. Review and describe the steps to the "Power-Struggle Shuffle."

4. Once a power struggle starts, you have three choices: step up, step back, or step over. Which do you choose most often? Why?

5. Give some examples of when you decided it would be best to step up, step back, or step over.

Notes

1. Foster Cline and Jim Fay, *Parenting by Love and Logic: Teaching Children Responsibility* (Colorado Springs: Pinon Press, 1990), 12.
2. Gary Smalley and John Trent, *The Gift of the Blessing* (Nashville: Thomas Nelson Publishers, 1993), 30–48.
3. *Webster's New World Dictionary,* College ed., s.v. "respect."
4. Donna Warner Manczak, "Raising Your Child's Self-Esteem," http://www.parenting.org; "Build Self-worth In Your Child," http://www.parenting.org; Jackie Connor, "Building Self-esteem in Children," www.ext.colostate.edu/pubs/columncc/cc960-530.html.
5. Donna Warner Manczak, "Raising Your Child's Self-Esteem," http://www.parenting.org; "Effective Praise: Applaud the Effort, Not Just the Outcome," http://www.parenting.org; Gary Smalley and John Trent, *The Blessing* (Nashville: Thomas Nelson Publishers, 1986); Michael Riley, "Some Pointers on Building Self-esteem In Children," West Michigan Community Mental Health System Web site; Thomas Blake, "Instilling Self-Esteem in Our Children—A Quick Guide."
6. Bill Maier, "Time for Family," http://www.troubledwith.com.
7. Bill Maier, "Time for Family," http://www.troubledwith.com; Focus on the Family, "The Rewards of Spending More Time with Your Children," http://www.focusonyourchild.com/develop/art1-/A0000691.html; Jeanette Friesen, "TIPS: What Has Happened to Family Time?" http://nuforfamilies.unl.edu/Tips/2004/TTPScolumn24.htm.

8. Jeanette Friesen, "TIPS: What Has Happened to Family Time?" http://nuforfamilies.unl.edu/Tips/2004/TTPScolumn24.htm.

9. Candy Arrington, "Slow 'Em Down," http://www.troubledwith.com; "Parenting Smarter, not Harder," http://www.parenting.org; Bill Maier, "Time for Family," http://www.troubledwith.com; Jeanette Friesen, "TIPS: What Has Happened to Family Time?" http://nuforfamilies.unl.edu/Tips/-2004/TTPScolumn24.htm; Jan Faull, "Loving Your Child" http://familyfun.go.com/parenting/child/skills/feature/dony29falove/.

10. Zig Ziglar, *Raising Positive Kids in a Negative World* (Nashville: Thomas Nelson Publishers, 1985), 47.

11. Ruth Wilson, "Caring: It's Not a Lesson, It's a Way of Life," http://www.earlychildhood.com/articles/index.cfm?fuseaction=Article&A=262.

12. *Webster's New World Dictionary*, College ed., s.v. "conversation."

13. Gary Smalley and John Trent, *Leaving the Light On* (Sisters, OR: Multnomah Publishers, 1994).

14. Dr. Marilyn Heins, "Discipline Don'ts," http://www.parentkidsright.com//pt-disciplinedonts.html.

15. Dr. Marilyn Heins, "Master the Effective Command," http://www.parentkidsright.com/pt-effectivecommand.html.

Additional copies of *ESCAPING THE PARENT TRAP*
and other LIFE JOURNEY books
are available wherever good books are sold.

If you have enjoyed this book,
or if it has had an impact on your life,
we would like to hear from you.

Please contact us at:

LIFE JOURNEY BOOKS
Cook Communications Ministries, Dept. 201
4050 Lee Vance View
Colorado Springs, CO 80918

Or visit our Web site: www.cookministries.com